# The Dead Sea Scrolls

# The Dead Sea Scrolls

*What Have We Learned?*

Eileen M. Schuller

Westminster John Knox Press
LOUISVILLE • LONDON

First published in Great Britain in 2006 by SCM Press
St Mary's Works, St Mary's Plain,
Norwich, Norfolk, NR3 3BH

*First American edition*
Published by Westminster John Knox Press
Louisville, Kentucky

PRINTED IN GREAT BRITAIN

06 07 08 09 10 11 12 13 14 15 — 10 9 8 7 6 5 4 3 2 1

Library of Congress Cataloging-in-Publication Data is on
file at the Library of Congress, Washington, D.C.

ISBN-13: 978-0-664-23112-5
ISBN-10: 0-664-23112-8

# Contents

114972

This book originates from a four-week lecture series given by the author at the University of Victoria, Canada.

SCM Press wishes to thank the Centre for Studies in Religion and Society at the University of Victoria and the organizers of the John Albert Hall Lecture Series.

# Preface and Acknowledgements

This book contains a slightly expanded version of the John Albert Hall Lectures I delivered at the University of Victoria in October 2002, under the title 'What Have We Learned from the Dead Sea Scrolls?' In revising the four oral presentations for this book, the first, Chapter 1, has been expanded considerably, and now incorporates and updates some material that was originally prepared as the presidential address to the Canadian Society of Biblical Studies in June 1995. The final pages are a brief addition to the lectures and look forward to areas of research and questions to be asked in the future. In this written text, I have still maintained something of the more personal style of the oral presentation.

I wish to take this opportunity to express my thanks to the many people involved in making these lectures possible. I am grateful above all to Dr Harold Coward and the John Albert Hall Lectures Committee who honoured me with the invitation. They took the risk that a topic that might have seemed either too sensationalistic or too specialized could be presented in a non-technical but academic way to the diverse general audience for whom this lectureship is intended. When the invitation was presented in the fall of 2000, I had just become Chair of the Department of Religious Studies at McMaster University and had to work around the demands of that job in addition to my own teaching. The flexibility of the organizers in allowing me to make two trips out to Victoria over a two-week period is what made it possible for me to accept. I am grateful for the help offered by Dr Conrad Brunck, Director of the Centre for Studies in Religion and Society, and Connie Carter, Administrator of the Centre, in arranging all the practical details, and for the kind and gracious hospitality of everyone at the Centre during my time in Victoria.

Although not a part of these published lectures, one of the responsibilities of the John Albert Hall lecturer is to give a 'Clergy Seminar' for the Diocese of British Columbia and interested guests. I want to express a special thank you to all who attended the day in which we studied together two recent documents in Jewish–Christian relationships (*Dabru Emet* and *A Sacred Obligation*) and explored their implications for pastoral ministry, especially during the season of Advent. The memory of the depth and intensity of our discussion remains one of the highlights of my time in Victoria.

This series of lectures drew upon and synthesized many talks that I have given on the Dead Sea Scrolls to both academic and non-academic audiences over the past 20 years. One of the unanticipated benefits of working on the scrolls is that I have been invited to share my research with numerous different groups of people who have a special interest in the scrolls or who simply want to learn something about whatever it is that is causing all the fuss in the media. I hesitate to name specific audiences, both because of their numbers and because I cannot include everyone, and yet I want to acknowledge how influential all these speaking occasions have been in shaping my own thoughts about the scrolls and their significance. Special mention should be made, however, of the opportunity to give

## *Preface and Acknowledgements*

the Robinson T. Orr Lectures at Huron University College (London, Ontario) and the Convocation Address at Concordia University College (Edmonton) where the material in Chapter 3 was first presented. Since the Victoria lectures, I have revised some of the material in light of presentations made to the Sunday Morning Breakfast Group at Anshe Shalom Synagogue (Hamilton), the Public Library (in London, Ontario), the Department of Classics (Concordia University, Montreal), the Ratisbonne Lecture Series (Saskatoon), and the Museum of Civilizations (Ottawa) lecture series in conjunction with the 'Ancient Treasures and the Dead Sea Scrolls' exhibit in early 2004.

For assistance in preparing the book manuscript I am grateful to Wayne Baxter, a graduate student in Religious Studies at McMaster University. These lectures are dedicated to the memory of my father, Norbert Schuller, who suffered a stroke just at the time they were delivered and died on 5 June 2003. As a carpenter and a construction worker all his life, my father's world was very different from the world of the scribe, whether the ancient scribes of Qumran or modern university professors. But as Ben Sira, the scribe *par excellence*, acknowledged over two thousand years ago, the artisans and workers – like my father – who 'rely on their hands and are skilful in their trade' are the ones who 'keep stable the fabric of our world' (Sira 38.31–4).

Eileen Schuller,
Hamilton, Ontario
April 2005

# Abbreviations

| | |
|---|---|
| BAR | *Biblical Archaeology Review* |
| BASOR | *Bulletin of the American Schools of Oriental Research* |
| CBQ | *Catholic Biblical Quarterly* |
| DJD | *Discoveries in the Judaean Desert* |
| DJDJ | *Discoveries in the Judaean Desert of Jordan* |
| DSD | *Dead Sea Discoveries* |
| ET | *Expository Times* |
| JJS | *Journal of Jewish Studies* |
| JSJ | *Journal for the Study of Judaism* |
| PAPS | *Proceedings of the American Philosophical Society* |
| RB | *Revue Biblique* |
| RQ | *Revue de Qumrân* |

There is a convention of numbering and abbreviations for the scrolls. The initial number indicates the cave where a particular scroll was found; Q = Qumran; the next number is the number assigned to the scroll, for example, 4Q502. This is followed by column number (or fragment number) and line numbers. Thus 4Q504 12 1 = from Qumran cave 4, scroll number 504, column 12, line 1.

Certain major scrolls are generally referred to by the first letter of their name (often the Hebrew name) rather than by number. A raised letter indicates multiple copies (for example, 1QS = the copy of the *Rule of the Community*, found in cave 1; 4QS$^b$ = the second copy of the *Rule of the Community* found in cave 4).

Occasionally different names are used for the same scroll, for example, the *Rule of the Community* was called in earlier years the *Manual of Discipline*.

| | |
|---|---|
| 1QS | *Rule of the Community* (Hebrew: *Serek*) |
| 1QM | *War Scroll* (Hebrew: *Milhamah*) |
| 1QH | *Thanksgiving Psalms* (Hebrew: *Hodayot*) |
| 1QapGen | *Genesis Apocryphon* |
| 4QD | *Damascus Document* |
| CD | *Cairo Damascus Document* (the copy of the *Damascus Document* discovered in a genizah [repository for old scrolls] in Cairo in 1896) |
| 11QT | *Temple Scroll* |
| 11QapocrPs | *Apocryphal Psalms* |

# Introduction

We begin by posing a question: 'What have we learned from the Dead Sea Scrolls after 50-plus years?' This formulation highlights the distinctive orientation of these lectures (and now this book). I am not presenting brand-new discoveries, but rather a discovery made over 50 years ago that everyone has heard at least something about already. Nor will I attempt to give a comprehensive and complete survey of all the Dead Sea Scrolls, with lists of documents, contents, origins and history. Fortunately we have a number of standard introductory handbooks that do just that; the reader can consult these excellent works for such information.[1] And nothing can substitute for actually reading the scrolls themselves, fortunately now available in good English translations.[2]

My goal is much more restricted. In the first chapter, I will take the reader through the past 50 years, decade by decade, and highlight the key events and accomplishments in scrolls scholarship. The three core chapters will each concentrate on a specific area where the scrolls have made a distinctive contribution to how we think about key questions in the development of early Judaism and early Christianity. In each chapter we will look at a few specific passages so as to become familiar with the actual text of the scrolls themselves, but I make no attempt to be comprehensive and to cover all the relevant works preserved at Qumran. Chapter 2 will explore what we have learned from the scrolls about the Scriptures and how biblical writings were formed and transmitted. Chapter 3 will examine some of the prayers, hymns and liturgies found in the scrolls and their significance for our understanding of the development of Jewish and Christian worship. Chapter 4 will draw on both texts and archaeological materials to demonstrate that – contrary to certain early claims that this was a male, celibate, even misogynist group – the scrolls in fact do provide considerable information about women. Finally, in a brief concluding chapter, I will make a few comments about directions for future research.

It is now over 50 years since the first rumours of a serendipitous, totally unexpected discovery of a cache of ancient manuscripts in desert caves first circulated through Jerusalem in the chaotic months as the British Mandate drew to a close in the spring of 1947.[3] In our culture, there is something special about the experience of 'turning 50' (one need only look at the self-help manuals in any bookstore, or the Hallmark greeting cards to see the virtual industry that has grown up around 'turning 50'), and the world of the Dead Sea Scrolls did not escape this phenomenon. In 1997, there was a whole series of academic conferences held literally around the world – in England, in Germany, at the annual meeting of the Society of Biblical Literature in San Francisco, and most significantly, in Jerusalem and at the site of Qumran itself.[4] All these events celebrated the fiftieth anniversary of that day in the winter of 1946–47 when a shepherd boy threw a stone into the cave and hit a clay jar and found, not the treasure of hidden gold he had hoped for, but a treasure of a different kind.

The fall of 2002 (when these lectures were originally

given) marked another half-century anniversary. It was mid-September 1952 that the Bedouin discovered the cave that we now know as cave 4, really two man-made caves in the soft marl terrace opposite the site of the ruins. By late fall 1952, thousands of small fragments were being offered for sale in the markets of the Old City and at the Palestine Archaeological Museum in East Jerusalem. For the first time, scholars were glimpsing something of the sheer amount of material that had been discovered and the magnitude of the task to publish these finds (the remains of over 550 manuscripts from cave 4 alone) in a way that would make them accessible for scholarly research for generations to come. Just short of 50 years later, in November 2001, celebrations were held at the Society of Biblical Literature meeting in Denver, Colorado to mark the completion of this project. There is now an official series of publications, *Discoveries in the Judaean Desert (DJD)*, 39 volumes from Oxford University Press that contain photos, transcriptions, translations, introductions, and a brief commentary on every manuscript (and even a volume including only 'Unidentified Fragments'). Having reached this major milestone, it is an appropriate time to step back and assess what we have learned from this mass of material.

Research in the Dead Sea Scrolls might seem a very specialized and circumscribed area, a minor sub-category within the whole discipline of Biblical Studies. For a field of study that was non-existent prior to 1946, the sheer volume of writing is now immense. A bibliography of scholarly books and articles over 25 years from 1970 to 1995 has some 5,600 entries; the comparable bibliography from 1995 to 2000 an additional 3,000 items.[5] An electronic bibliography, updated weekly by Orion Center at Hebrew University, Jerusalem, adds some five to ten items per week on average.[6] There are two scholarly journals devoted specifically to the Dead Sea Scrolls, *Revue de Qumrân*, established already in 1958, and the more recent *Dead Sea Discoveries*, begun in 1994. There are now sub-specialties, and most scholars focus on a specific and limited body of texts (halakhic, biblical, liturgical); it is now almost impossible for one person to be an expert in every field of Dead Sea Scrolls research or to have read everything being written. In these pages, we can only scratch the surface, but hopefully this brief and selective treatment of certain issues will give readers some sense both of what we have learned and what remains to be learned from these complex but fascinating documents.

## Notes

Full details on books and chapters mentioned in the notes will be found in the Select Bibliography at the end of the book.

1. Full-length recent introductions to the Dead Sea Scrolls include: James C. VanderKam and Peter Flint, *The Meaning of the Dead Sea Scrolls*; James C. VanderKam, *The Dead Sea Scrolls Today*; Lawrence H. Schiffman, *Reclaiming the Dead Sea Scrolls*; Geza Vermes, *An Introduction to the Complete Dead Sea Scrolls*. For an older 'classic' introduction that has been updated: Frank Moore Cross, *The Ancient Library of Qumran*.

2. In terms of the selection of the texts, reasonable cost, and the inclusion of a full introduction, I would suggest that the reader start with Geza Vermes, *The Complete Dead Sea Scrolls in English*. This is the translation that will be used throughout this volume, unless otherwise indicated. Other English translations include: Michael Wise, Martin Abegg and Edward Cook, *The Dead Sea Scrolls: A New Translation*; Florentino García Martínez and Eibert Tigchelaar, *The Dead Sea Scrolls Study Edition*.

3. The actual date of the discovery is still a matter of some dispute. It has been variously reported as November–December 1946 or January–

# Introduction

February 1947. The Bedouin, of course, were not keeping records according to our calendar, but these were the months when the Taamireh Bedouin were traditionally in this area with their flocks and, in the earliest oral accounts, Muhammad ed-Deeb mentions wearing a cloak, as would be expected in the winter cold.

4. The papers from most of these conferences have been published and, although often somewhat technical and academic, these volumes provide an overview of the current state of scholarship. Robert A. Kugler and Eileen M. Schuller (eds), *The Dead Sea Scrolls at Fifty*, the papers from the Society of Biblical Literature Qumran Section fiftieth anniversary special session; Lawrence H. Schiffman, Emanuel Tov and James C. VanderKam (eds), *The Dead Sea Scrolls Fifty Years After Their Discovery 1947–1997*, 96 papers from the Jerusalem conference.

5. Florentino García Martínez and Donald W. Parry, *A Bibliography of the Finds in the Desert of Judah 1970–95*; Avital Pinnick, *The Orion Center Bibliography of the Dead Sea Scrolls (1995–2000)*.

6. The website of the Orion Center for the Study of the Dead Sea Scrolls and Associated Literature is a valuable resource for scrolls information for both scholars and the general reader: http://orion.mscc. huji.ac.il. The Shrine of the Book at the Israel Museum also has a website for the general reader: http://www.imj.org.il/eng/shrine.

I

# Fifty Years Plus:
# A Survey Decade by Decade

The saga of the discovery of a cave with unexpected content near the western shore of the Dead Sea, and the series of events that this discovery set in motion, has been told and retold many times. A number of the key players involved in the very early years have left us their personal memoirs.[1] Less attention has been paid to how events unfolded over the long haul, as the decades passed by. Indeed, for some years the Dead Sea Scrolls seemed to disappear from public interest, only to return briefly to the spotlight at sporadic intervals because of some new find, or crisis, or scandal.

The full story of the past 50 years of scrolls research remains to be written.[2] In this chapter I can give only a brief and selective overview of this half century, focusing on key events of particular importance in understanding how and why the study of the scrolls took the path that it has. I will use two very early announcements about the discovery from 1948 as my starting point, and attempt to draw out the implications of what was said then in the light of subsequent developments. I will traipse lightly through a half century, stopping to pause briefly – and somewhat arbitrarily – at ten-year intervals

(1957, 1967 and so on) to take our bearings and survey what has been accomplished. Any overview like this is by definition highly selective, and to that extent an interpretation, and I am sure that some of my own biases and judgements will all too soon be revealed. But as we make this journey we will meet many of the key players and hopefully come to some understanding of the state of research at the beginning of the sixth decade.

## The First Announcements

On 11 April 1948, the American School of Oriental Research issued a short press release that appeared the next day in *The Times* of London:

> Yale University announced yesterday the discovery in Palestine of the earliest known manuscript of the book of Isaiah. It was found in the Syrian monastery of St Mark in Jerusalem, where it had been preserved in a scroll of parchment dating to about the first century BC. Recently it was identified by scholars of the American School of Oriental Research in Jerusalem.
>
> There were also examined at the school three other ancient Hebrew scrolls. One was part of a commentary on the book of Habakkuk; another seemed to be a manual of discipline of some comparatively little-known sect or monastic order, possibly the Essenes. The third scroll has not been identified.

This succinct, rather staid, initial announcement already said a great deal, especially when we look at it from the perspective of half a century of further developments:

*Scrolls*: This was, above all, a discovery of ancient written documents. There were some artefacts (distinctively shaped clay jars, linen wrappings) recovered from the first cave, and eventually the extensive ruins of buildings nearby would be excavated by archaeologists, but this was, above all, a discovery of written documents, the remains of approximately 900 manuscripts.

*Hebrew scrolls*: While it was to be expected that the book of Isaiah would be in Hebrew, and that a commentary on the prophet Habakkuk might be in Hebrew, it was more surprising to find a non-biblical work concerned with daily life and community organization written in the sacred tongue. Clearly Hebrew was still a living language for composition and probably also for speech; it had not been totally replaced by Aramaic. What was not known at the time of this announcement was that the unidentified scroll (the *Genesis Apocryphon*) is in Aramaic, as are about 120 other scrolls (just under 15 per cent of the total).

*Dating about the first century BC*: The date of first century BC for this copy of the book of Isaiah was determined on palaeographic grounds; that is, by comparison of the handwriting with the writing of inscriptions, particularly on ossuaries from around Jerusalem, and with a few other surviving written documents such as the Nash Papyrus from Egypt. Some scrolls from other caves have now been dated as early as the beginning of the second century BC and a few as late as mid-first century AD, but the largest number were copied in the first century BC.

**Content of the scrolls:** These four scrolls are typical of what would be found in the collection as a whole. The book of Isaiah, of course, had long been known and studied as one of the books of the Hebrew Bible (Old Testament), but now we had a copy at least 1,000 years earlier than any previously known copy.[3] The other scrolls contained materials unknown previous to this discovery. The second, the *Commentary on Habakkuk*, illustrates a genre seen for the first time at Qumran, with individual biblical verses quoted serially, followed by an explanation (*pesher*) of the meaning of each verse, basically the same format as in a modern commentary. The unidentified scroll, when it was finally opened with great difficulty some years later, turned out to be a retelling and expansion of parts of the biblical book of Genesis, especially the sections about the birth of Noah, the flood, and Abraham and Sarah in Egypt; hence the name given to it, the *Genesis Apocryphon*. This is an example of a rich group of texts that retell and reinterpret biblical materials, thus providing a window into how the Scriptures were being read and understood. The other scroll is not related so specifically to the Bible. It contains various elements: a liturgical ceremony of blessings and curses and a long poetic hymn; statements of belief and theology ('From the God of knowledge comes all that is and shall be . . . He has created man to govern the world, and appointed for him two spirits in which to walk'); and detailed rules and regulations for the governance of a community, including a penal code listing specific punishments for violation of specified norms. The work was given the title the *Manual of Discipline* because it reminded some of the Christian scholars who were reading this sort of material for the first time of their own books of church polity (for example, the Methodist *Manual of Discipline*). It is now called the *Rule of the Community,* and is only one of a number of such rules (along with the *Rule of the Congregation,* and the *Damascus Document*).

***Some comparatively little-known sect or monastic order:*** In modern sociological terms, the people who wrote the *Rule of the Community* demonstrated certain characteristics of a 'sect'. Like other Jews, they followed the law of Moses, but they claimed that they alone knew how to interpret it correctly; they were the Sons of Light surrounded by the Sons of Darkness. The withdrawal into the desert, communal sharing of property, strict community organization and rules, and above all the absence of any mention of women and children suggested that we had here some sort of predecessor to the Christian monastic orders that would flourish in the same wilderness a few centuries later.

***Possibly the Essenes:*** Descriptions of Second Temple Judaism (from the historian Josephus, the New Testament, later rabbinic sources) spoke of distinctive 'sects' or 'schools': the Pharisees, the Sadducees and the Essenes. Even on the basis of what was known from these first scrolls, the authors were clearly not the Pharisees; the Qumran group had a different, even stricter interpretation of the Torah, which was based not on Oral Torah given on Mount Sinai but on the ongoing revelation granted to their leader and founder, the Teacher of Righteousness. Although their leaders were priests (and called themselves 'the sons of Zadok'), these were not the Sadducees; they believed in angels and resurrection, or at least some form of life after death. But there were many similarities with the Essenes as described by Josephus, Philo and Pliny: they lived a community life with a strict hierarchial structure, shared property in common, and did not mention marriage, women or children; even specific and minor details matched, such as the prohibition against spitting in the assembly.[4] Though other elements did not fit so well (the exact process of initiation, and especially the strong apocalyptic and eschatological emphasis found in the scrolls), a possible link between the scrolls and the Essenes seemed logical to scholars already by the time of this very first announcement.

Before we leave this newspaper clipping, we can note how this brief announcement is itself a microcosm of the complexity of the concrete political and religious circumstances of the find: Jewish scrolls, discovered in Palestine just at the end of the British Mandate rule, in the possession of the Syrian (Christian Orthodox) monastery of St Mark, made public by the American Schools of Oriental Research at Yale University in the United States. And, as with almost every press announcement about the scrolls over the next 50 years, it is in part accurate and informative, and in part misleading, incomplete and simply wrong. The book of Isaiah was not 'found' in the Syrian monastery of St Mark and no mention is made of the cave in the Judean desert or how the scroll made its way to Jerusalem.

As so often happens, media publicity brings forth new information. A few days later, on 26 April 1948, Dr Eleazer Sukenik, the president of Hebrew University, issued another press release not only to correct some details, but to announce that, unbeknown to the monks at St Mark's or the scholars at the American School, there were three more scrolls. In late November 1947, in the last tumultuous days of the British Mandate, he had taken the Arab bus to Bethlehem and purchased from an antiquities dealer a second, more fragmentary, copy of the book of Isaiah, a collection of psalmic-like poetry that he called the *Thanksgiving Scroll*, and the *War Scroll*, which contained a detailed battle plan for the eschatological war of Sons of Light versus the Sons of Darkness. These scrolls belonged now to the Hebrew University of Jerusalem.

## W. F. Albright: 'An Absolutely Incredible Find'

W. F. Albright, perhaps the senior and most respected of Old Testament scholars and palaeographers in North America, was immediately sent some of the very first photographs of the scrolls, which had been taken at the Albright Institute in February 1948. In a famous letter written on 15 March 1948, and in an article in the *Bulletin of the American Schools of Oriental Research* in April, Albright pronounced his verdict on the significance of the find:

> My heartiest congratulations on the greatest MS discovery of modern times! . . . You can imagine how my eyes bulged when I saw the script through my magnifying glass! What an absolutely incredible find! The new discovery will revolutionize Intertestamental studies . . . it will soon antiquate all present handbooks on the background of the New Testament and on the textual criticism and interpretation of the Old Testament.[5]

What, really, was so astounding and revolutionary? It is not that the scrolls were chronologically so old. Since the nineteenth century, the archaeological world had been dazzled by much older finds, hundreds of thousands of clay texts from Babylon, the hieroglyphs on the walls of the tombs of Egypt, some going back to the third and second millennium BC; in

7

comparison 100 BC is not old at all. The tablets of Babylon had been written on hard, sun-baked clay, the Egyptian hieroglyphs on the walls of carefully constructed sealed tombs. But in the land of Israel, apart from a few inscriptions on stone (for example, Hezekiah's Tunnel Inscription, names on limestone burial ossuaries), most writing was done on animal skins that had been partially tanned (technically not quite parchment) and on sheets of papyrus made from plant reeds from Egypt. These are fragile materials, easily destroyed by use and time, even more so by rain, mildew and the gnawing of rats and bats. Virtually no manuscripts from Palestine had survived that were written before approximately AD 1000.

Thus the physical survival of scrolls from a millennium earlier was itself a wonder no matter what they might have contained. Unlike the thousands of mundane economic texts (bills of sale, tax receipts) from Babylonia, these are almost all religious texts. In the collection as a whole, approximately one quarter of the scrolls are copies of the books of the Hebrew Bible. A much smaller number are copies of other Jewish books that we had known in later translations (Ethiopic, Slavonic) because they were preserved by various Christian churches, now found in the original Hebrew and Aramaic (books like Ben Sira, Tobit, *Enoch* and *Jubilees*). Two thirds are works that had not been known prior to their discovery at Qumran. So much more of the Jewish religious literature from the Second Temple period now became accessible to us.

Albright claimed that this material would change our understanding of 'the background of the New Testament', the so-called 'Intertestamental Period' between the Old Testament and the New Testament. Again, it was not that we previously knew nothing of Judaism under the Greek and Roman Empires, the world from which Christianity emerged. We had

had the books of 1 and 2 Maccabees, which gave a detailed picture of the traumatic crisis in the mid-second century BC when Judaism fought for its very existence in the face of Greek persecution until the family of the Maccabees rose up, filled with holy zeal for God's law, to cast off the Greek yoke by a combination of military battles and diplomacy and eventually to become high priests and kings – all under the plan of God according to the books of Maccabees. From the book of Daniel, we could hear a slightly different theological perspective: in this time of crisis, deliverance would come from direct divine intervention, with at best 'a little help' from human agents (Dan. 11.34). For subsequent history under the Roman Empire up to the Jewish revolt of AD 66–70, we depended largely on the detailed accounts of Josephus, a Jewish participant in the revolt, writing under Roman patronage after the final defeat. We also had some philosophical works from the Diaspora, especially the long series of treatises from Philo of Alexandria. There were more apocalyptic books like *1 Enoch*, *4 Ezra* and *2 Baruch*, which had not been included in the 'canon' of Scripture and reflected the hopes and expectations of less mainstream groups.

Early in the twentieth century, R. H. Charles had collected much of this material for the first time in English (in his two-volume work, *The Apocrypha and Pseudepigrapha of the Old Testament*) but few scholars paid much attention to such 'fringe' works that survived on the periphery. In the standard textbooks, Judaism of the Second Temple period was viewed through the lens of Josephus, the New Testament and the rabbis. The Pharisees were dominant and their rulings and interpretation of the Law prevailed; the Sadducees were occupied mainly with the temple and in keeping on good terms with the Romans; there may have been Essenes, some sort of mysterious, esoteric group, or perhaps this was just a utopian invention to show that Jews could be just as philosophical and ascetic as Greeks. Albright was right that handbooks would now have to be rewritten, because in the scrolls we were hearing for the first time another voice. In the *Commentary on Habakkuk*, we hear from Jews who viewed the Maccabees not as glorious saviours, but as Wicked Priests, men of debauchery and illegal wealth, who usurped the priesthood and seized control of the temple. Even when we had only the materials from cave 1, it was clear that the scrolls were reflecting a situation of bitter conflicts over the priesthood, the temple, the interpretation of Torah and the calendar (for example, in the *Commentary on Habakkuk* the Wicked Priest seems to celebrate the Day of Atonement on a different day than the authors of the commentary). Clearly first-century Judaism was more diverse and more complex than scholars had assumed.

Given that these newly discovered texts were written in the first century, close to the time framework of Jesus, and came geographically from the wilderness of Judea, the very area associated in the gospels with John the Baptist, it was but a small step to expect that the scrolls would tell us something about John, Jesus and the beginnings of Christianity. Would they reveal details of the 'hidden years of Jesus'? Had Jesus been at Qumran? Might we recover from the caves a new gospel, or a Hebrew/Aramaic version of the existing gospels, or even very early Greek copies of the gospels, unspoiled by centuries of scribal copying? How close were the similarities between the scrolls and the New Testament, between Jesus and the Teacher of Righteousness? Was there some truth in the claim that the 'birthplace of Christianity was not Nazareth, but the caves of Qumran'? True, there was nothing like this in the materials discovered so far, but the anticipation, the expectation of what might be found sparked the interest and excitement both of devout Christians who looked for a confirmation of their faith and of sceptics who sought evidence to discredit the Christian claims.

## The First Decade: 1947–57

Let us leap immediately from these announcements in 1948 to the spring of 1957, and put the question: What happened in the first ten years? What had we learned ten years after the initial discovery? Looking back from today's perspective, we can appreciate the truly astonishing progress and accomplishments of that first decade.

By 1957, all of the seven scrolls from cave 1, with photos, transcriptions and translations, were available to scholars throughout the world. Sukenik had released some of the better preserved *Thanksgiving Psalms* already in 1948 and 1950 in Hebrew, and these were quickly translated into various languages (one of the first to appear was a Latin version in 1950![6]). Before his death in 1953, Sukenik prepared for publication the three scrolls in his possession: Isaiah[b], the *Thanksgiving Scroll* and the *War Scroll* in both Hebrew and English in 1954/55.[7] The four scrolls in the possession of St Mark's Monastery were taken to the United States in 1948 and languished there until they were sold to Israel in 1954, but the excellent photos taken by John Trever were published already in 1950/51.[8] By 1957 editions of all these major texts, many with full commentary, were readily available in most modern languages. This fact needs emphasis, since in the exuberance over the 'release of the scrolls' post-1990, sometimes the impression is given that virtually nothing had been available to scholars earlier.

In addition, by 1957, all the other caves in the immediate vicinity that contained written material had been explored.[9] The actual location of cave 1 was discovered early in 1949 by the Jordanian Department of Antiquities, who conducted a scientific exploration of the cave and recovered considerable materials left behind by the Bedouin – fragments of 72 manuscripts and some 67 jars and jar covers. The ten other caves with written materials were discovered either by archaeologists or, most often, by the Bedouin who knew the desert so much better. Cave 4 deserves special mention. Archaeologists had paid little attention to the marl terrace just above the ruins, but the Bedouin remembered the elders talking of an opening into the 'Cave of the Partridge' which they found in August 1952. Inside what was really two artificially made caves, the Bedouin found by far the largest cache, literally thousands of small, badly damaged pieces scattered on the cave floor, not a single rolled scroll as in cave 1, and none wrapped in linen or placed in jars.

With the exception of the *Temple Scroll* from cave 11 (found in 1956 and hidden by an antiquities dealer for another ten years), virtually all of the fragments from the 11 caves (close to 50,000 pieces in total) were in the hands of the Jordanian Department of Antiquities by 1957.[10] Within weeks of the discovery of cave 4, the Bedouin started bringing shoeboxes and bags stuffed full of fragments to the École Biblique and the Palestine Archaeological Museum. The Jordanian government set aside 15,000 dinars, and material was purchased at the set price of 1 dinar (roughly $2.80) per square centimetre (to stop the Bedouin from tearing the fragments further to get more pieces!). A preliminary, but surprisingly comprehensive, survey of all the material was quickly compiled by 1956.[11] The materials from the other caves fell into basically the same categories as what was found in cave 1: biblical texts; copies of previously known apocryphal and pseudepigraphic books; and previously unknown works: hymns and prayers, calendrical texts, biblical interpretation, wisdom reflections, legal rulings, and a few more esoteric bits (for example, divination texts such as a horoscope and brontology; the list of hidden treasure on the *Copper Scroll*).

The Jordanian government quickly realized that it lacked both the financial and human resources to deal with the enormity of this find. To supply the latter, a call went out to academic institutions throughout the world, to send young scholars to work in Jerusalem, and these formed the so-called 'International Team': Józef T. Milik (Polish/French), Maurice Baillet and Jean Starcky (French); Claus-Hunno Huntzinger (German); Frank Moore Cross and Patrick Skehan (American), John Allegro and John Strugnell (British), under the leadership of Roland de Vaux from the École Biblique. In our more ecumenical times, it is easy to forget that one of the revolutionary aspects of the composition of this International Team was that Catholic and Protestant scholars were actually working together on the Bible; a 1957 feature article in the Canadian edition of *Time* magazine described the group rather quaintly as 'an international – and inter-creedal – task force of scholars'.[12] Jewish scholars on the other side of the Mandelbaum Gate could take no part, though it is well known that Yigael Yadin and Roland de Vaux communicated steadily throughout these years via a postal box in Europe.

By 1957, a group of scholars was daily at work sorting, matching, cataloguing, mounting and making a first reading of the thousands of pieces spread out on long tables in 'the

Scrollery' of the Museum. In a very real way – too often not explicitly acknowledged – their labours laid the foundation for all future study of the scrolls. Although occasionally new joins can still be made (usually of very small pieces), the passage of 40 years has affected colour, texture and shrinkage in the material (whether animal skins or papyrus), and joins and divisions made today are usually less certain. The highly skilled Armenian photographer, Najib Anton Albina, produced a truly excellent set of photographs that still remains indispensable for readings; the quality of his work has not been equalled even in the more recent sets of photos taken with much more sophisticated equipment by the Israeli Department of Antiquities and foreign photographers.[13]

This first decade also brought five seasons of archaeological work at the site of the ruins near the caves under the direction of Roland de Vaux of the École Biblique et Archéologique Française and G. Lankester Harding of the Jordanian Department of Antiquities. De Vaux's interpretation of the site as a communal living centre from the second half of the second century BC until its violent destruction by the Roman Legions in AD 68/69 was given wide publicity when he gave the Schweich Lectures at the British Academy in London in 1959.[14] After a fierce but short-lived 'battle' about date (whether the scrolls were really ancient or medieval), the results of carbon 14 testing on linen found in cave 1 corroborated palaeographic analysis to fix the chronological parameters from approximately the second century BC to the first century AD.

In addition to all this, the larger task of providing a framework of interpretation was well advanced by 1957. As we saw earlier (pp. 2–6 above), the first press release from the American Schools of Oriental Research had already suggested a link between this new 'sect or monastic order' and the Essenes. Geza Vermes, in his doctoral dissertation in 1953, outlined the main shape of what has come to be designated the 'consensus-theory' or 'the Essene hypothesis' and this was popularized in two books from 1957 and 1958 by J. T. Milik and F. M. Cross.[15] The authors of the scrolls were seen as a dissident Jewish group that came into being in the aftermath of the Hellenistic struggle in mid-second century BC, in opposition to the Hasmoneans over issues of priesthood and calendar. Influenced by the descriptions of Josephus and Philo as much as by the scrolls themselves, the Essene hypothesis emphasized certain features such as celibacy and a communal (monastic) lifestyle, though recognizing important elements of eschatological fervour and messianic expectation that were barely mentioned in the classical descriptions of the Essenes. But other voices and interpretations were also making themselves heard. For almost every one of the alternate theories of scroll origins put forth (sometimes with great fanfare and claims for originality) in the last few years, one can find antecedents in dissenting ideas already circulating by the end of this first decade, claims that the authors of the scrolls were really Sadducees, or Pharisees, or Zealots, or an unnamed *sui generis* group, or Christians.

The years 1947–57 saw more than their share of wild speculation about the relationship between the scrolls, Essenes and Christianity – everything from the 'did Jesus live at Qumran?' question to claims that the Teacher of Righteousness had been crucified, even resurrected. The decade ended with the publication of a major collection of essays, *The Scrolls and the New Testament*, a volume that was reissued in paperback some 35 years later (1992) because it still served to define the key areas for discussion of the interrelationship between the scrolls and

New Testament studies: eschatological expectation, messianism, communal meals, church discipline, theological vocabulary, the role of John the Baptist.[16] New texts, especially some published in the last ten years, can supplement this volume, but the basic issues of the scrolls and Christianity were already articulated here.

By 1957, the significance of the approximately 200 biblical manuscripts had been recognized, even though only a few had been fully published. As Albright had intuited already in his 1948 letter (p. 7 above), the entire discipline of textual criticism would have to be rethought on the basis of so much new evidence about the Hebrew texts and the versions prior to the standardization of the Masoretic text. It was reading the Samuel manuscripts in the early 1950s (particularly 4QSam[a,b], copies that diverged from the Masoretic text and agreed with the Septuagint) that enabled Frank Moore Cross to formulate the basic outline of a radically new theory about the geographical origin of local texts. And, on a more practical level, Millar Burrows, during the sea voyage home from Israel in the summer of 1948, correlated the large Isaiah manuscript against the Masoretic text so that the results could be considered by the Revision Committee for the Revised Standard Version (RSV), who ultimately adopted 13 variant readings from the Isaiah Scroll for the RSV (1952).

The product of this first decade of scrolls study was some 1,550 scholarly books and articles by 616 authors in 22 languages.[17] The first issue of a new journal devoted solely to scrolls study, *Revue de Qumrân*, was in preparation. Oxford University Press established an official series, *Discoveries in the Judaean Desert* (*DJD*), to publish scholarly editions of all of the scrolls, and the first volume of fragments from cave 1 appeared in 1955. But the sheer volume of material, as well as its complexity, meant that the quick results of the first decade would be impossible to sustain. The words of Lankester Harding in the Foreword to the first volume of *DJD* proved to be prophetic: 'Work of this nature is of necessity slow, and it may well be a few years before the series can be completed.'

## The Second Decade: 1957–67

Let us leap ahead a decade now to spring 1967, and take a look around in the months just before the Six-Day War of June 1967. The members of the International Team had scattered to take up university posts in North America and Europe when the Rockefeller money that had been supporting them came to an end in the summer of 1960. From now on, most of the work on the scrolls would compete with (and often take a second place to) all the other demands of academic life and teaching. But before they dispersed, much had been accomplished. The fragments were sorted and laid out on glass plates (unfortunately individual pieces were affixed with scotch tape!); 620 plates of fragments were arranged and numbered, leaving only 25 plates with still unidentified fragments. Most of the fragments had already been read carefully, as evidenced by the hand-written cards that listed each word, that were prepared between 1957 and 1960. These cards, in a large tray, were kept in the 'Scrolls Room', accessible to team members who came to Jerusalem, and in 1988 were photographed and published privately; they served as an invaluable resource to many editors in preparing their texts for publication.

Slowly various scrolls were edited and made public, sometimes in preliminary versions in journal articles, so that in fact more texts were being read and discussed in these years than a list of official publications indicates.[18] The official *DJD* series expanded: *DJD* II (1961) published the finds from Wadi Murabba'at; *DJDJ* III (1962), the small caves 2–3, 5–10; *DJDJ* IV (1965), the cave 11 Psalms Scroll, a fascinating manuscript containing both biblical and non-biblical psalms that stimulated questions – still unresolved – about the very nature of a fixed biblical canon; and *DJD* V (submitted in 1966, published in 1968), the first volume of cave 4 materials, John Allegro's allotment of biblical interpretations and commentaries (*pesharim*). These years were a time of consolidation and the working out of basic insights from the previous decade: for example, the development of a full palaeographical typology which is still used today in dating the manuscripts,[19] and more specific studies on the relationship between the scrolls and the New Testament, especially Paul and John.[20]

The twentieth anniversary of the discovery attracted little fanfare, and even the Six-Day War in June 1967 brought little drastic change, at least on the surface. Fighting took place in the grounds of the Palestine Archaeological Museum. The Qumran materials had been taken from the Scrollery and crated for removal to Amman (though in fact they never left the museum); a few pieces, including a beautiful and very old 4QSam[b] fragment that was on display, seem to have disappeared at this time. Since the Jordanian government had nationalized the museum just months earlier (November 1966), the museum and the scrolls now came under the control of the Israeli Director of Antiquities who allowed the International Team to continue to function much as before.

## The Third Decade: 1967–77

This decade marked a low point in Qumran studies: the death
of Roland de Vaux in 1971, the appointment of a fellow
Dominican as editor of *DJD*, Pierre Benoit, who had worked
only peripherally with the scrolls, and the changed political
reality all played their part. The twenty-fifth anniversary in
1973 did spark a number of excellent review surveys, including one of the first articles to discuss the influence of the scrolls
on Jewish Studies specifically.[21] But no new *DJD* volumes
appeared until the very end of the decade (*DJD* VI, 1977); this
collection of *tefillin*, *mezuzot* and a few verses of a Leviticus
Targum failed to elicit much response and indirectly height-
ened the popular perception that the excitement and novelty
had gone out of Qumran studies. Milik's publication of the
Aramaic fragments of *Enoch* in 1976 and some of the far-
reaching theories he proposed in his mammoth volume
aroused considerable debate.[22] But what really captured
attention was the claim by the Spanish papyrologist, José
O'Callaghan, that some of the tiny Greek fragments found in
cave 7 might be in fact copies of New Testament texts.[23] The
popular media exploited the Christian connection, especially
claims that the discovery of bits of 1 Timothy, Acts, and even
2 Peter from as early as before AD 68 would mean that 'seven
tons of German NT scholarship could now be consigned
to the flames' (as one journalist put it rather vividly). The
identification of any cave 7 fragments with New Testament
passages has never been proven with any degree of certainty,
though the issue is revived periodically.[24]

Apart from a few such fireworks, the dominant sentiment in
1977 was that expressed by Michael Knibb of the University
of London in an article to mark the end of the third decade:

[It] is now some thirty years since the Dead Sea Scrolls were first discovered . . . there is nothing dramatic to report – no sensational new discovery, no brilliant new book which provides the key to the interpretation . . . The Scrolls have begun to sink into a relative scholarly obscurity, and this is all the more likely to be the case now that the discovery of the Ebla tablets has caught hold of the popular imagination.[25]

## The Fourth Decade: 1977–87

The next decade, 1977–87, was also a 'time of small things' (Zech. 4.10). The somnolence and isolation that had marked the previous decade continued, though the winds of change were stirring, sometimes in ways not recognizable until the gales lashed out in full force in the next decade. In the early 1980s we began to hear radically different theories about the origin of the scrolls and the community/communities who produced them. For example, Norman Golb denied that there was any integral connection between the ruins at the site of Khirbet Qumran (which he considered to be a Hasmonean fortress) and the scrolls that had been brought from the libraries of Jerusalem and hidden during the Jewish Revolt;[26] Robert Eisenman reconstructed a revolutionary, messianic movement that included John the Baptist, Jesus and James (as the Teacher of Righteousness), raging a fierce struggle against the power of the Empire and Paul (the Man of the Lie).[27] Golb's ideas have been debated seriously over the last 15 years and while he highlights a number of real problem areas in the more traditional reconstruction, his hypothesis likewise fails to account for the totality of the data; Eisenman has been successful in attracting the attention of a series of journalists who have given his ideas far more publicity in the popular media than they ever earned in scholarly circles.[28]

More productive new life came from new texts, especially the publication of the *Temple Scroll*. Physically the most massive of the Qumran scrolls (well over a metre longer than the complete book of Isaiah), the *Temple Scroll* describes in comprehensive detail regulations concerning the physical structure of the temple and its precincts, laws of sacrifice, ritual purity and impurity, festival offerings, laws of the king, witnesses, oaths, regulations for war and marriage. Acquired by Yigael Yadin during the Six-Day War, and published in Hebrew in 1977 and then in the more widely accessible English version in 1983,[29] this work remains – even today – one of the most enigmatic of the Qumran texts. But it was the *Temple Scroll* that served to bring into prominence two issues that have become increasingly central to Qumran studies: first, the crucial importance of the legal (halakhic) material in addition to the theological or eschatological passages that hitherto had been the focus of interest (particularly for Christian scholars); and second, the recognition that not all works found in the caves necessarily came from the same provenance. Although Yadin had assumed that the *Temple Scroll* was an Essene work, other scholars demonstrated significant differences in thought and in legal regulation that pointed to an origin in some other milieu (despite the scroll eventually finding its way into cave 11). A whole new discussion began to take shape: today it is often expressed in terms of a distinction between 'sectarian' works (those characterized by a distinctive terminology, ideological outlook, references to community structures and to the Teacher of Righteousness, avoidance of the Tetragrammaton) and 'non-sectarian' works (most often prayers, court tales, apocalypses, biblical retellings, many written in Aramaic) that exhibit none of the distinctive 'sectarian' features. These may have originated in 'mainstream Judaism', though they were considered important by the Qumran community and thus preserved in their library. These 'non-sectarian' works, many of which probably were composed in the fourth, third or early second centuries BC, are an important window into the late Persian and early Hellenistic period, a period of Judaism about which we have known so little.[30]

In 1982 a major new volume of *DJD* (VII) finally did appear. The introductory comments of the editor, Maurice Baillet, are well worth reading; it is an emotional, plaintive cry that conveys a sense of what it felt like to work so long and so hard over many years on literally thousands of the tiniest, most difficult fragments under arduous personal and political conditions. This volume included six or seven very fragmentary copies of the *War Scroll*, on first glance rather insignificant given that we had known since the 1950s the much more complete cave 1 copy of the *War Scroll*. Yet these were not simply copies, but very different versions of a *War Scroll*; it was now possible to glimpse something of the complex process of recensional activity and ideological revision that lay behind what we had simply known as 'the' *War Scroll*. Looking ahead, something of the same multi-layered process of composition, redaction and revision would become apparent when the cave 4 copies of the *Rule of the Community* (*DJD* XXVI, 1998) and of the *Thanksgiving Psalms* (*DJD* XXIX, 1999) were finally published. Clearly these key sectarian texts were all complex works, and scholars would need to develop more sophisticated ways to think about their literary development and the correlation between the world of the text and historical reality. Furthermore, it was with the publication of *DJD* VII that scholars first became aware of the amount and significance of yet another genre, the liturgical materials in the Qumran corpus. Baillet published collections of prayers for each day of the week (4Q504–506), prayers for each day of the month (4Q503), prayers for the major festivals (4Q507–509), hymns 'to terrify and frighten all the spirits . . . and demons' (4Q510–11), rituals for purification (4Q512) and a fascinating but very fragmentary text of some sort of liturgical service of rejoicing labelled (probably misleadingly) 'A Ritual of Marriage' (4Q502).

In the decade 1977–87, deliberate efforts were made to increase the number of people working on publication of the scrolls. John Strugnell became Benoit's deputy and then successor as editor-in-chief of the International Team. At Strugnell's initiative, the first of a new generation of Israeli scholars became involved in the work of publication (including Emanuel Tov, Elisha Qimron, Devorah Dimant), and both Strugnell and Cross began to entrust selected manuscripts to their graduate students to prepare the first edition. Thus, in this decade more new texts become available, not in the official *DJD* series, but as doctoral dissertations and preliminary publications.[31] Of particular impact was a brief paper, 'An Unpublished Halakhic Letter from Qumran' presented by Elisha Qimron and John Strugnell at the International Congress on Biblical Archaeology in Jerusalem in 1984.[32] Tremendous excitement was generated when it was announced that they were working on a document (4QMMT, *Miqsat Ma'aseh haTorah*) that could give us new information about the founding of the sect. In Qimron's words, here we had 'a letter from a leader of the Qumran sect (possibly the Teacher of Righteousness himself) to the leader of its opponents', detailing specific differences in the interpretation of the law between 'you' and 'we', with the result that 'we have separated ourselves from the majority of the peo[ple]'. Even more important than the contents per se of this newly released document was the sense of expectation that it aroused: if this was still unpublished, what else was there?

## The Fifth Decade: 1987–97

Once we arrive at 1987 and in the years following, the issues of accessibility and speed of publication take centre stage. Some years earlier, Geza Vermes of Oxford University had warned that 'unless drastic measures are taken at once, the greatest and most valuable of all the Hebrew and Aramaic manuscript discoveries is likely to become the academic scandal *par excellence* of the twentieth century'.[33] But in 1977 his words had scarcely caused a ripple. Yet, the passage of another ten years with little overt activity, the coming-of-age of a new generation of scrolls scholars, even the world political situation (these were the years leading up to *Glasnost* and the fall of the Berlin wall) meant that in the years following the fortieth anniversary, the 'academic scandal *par excellence*' became a fully-fledged drama, played out on the pages of *Biblical Archaeology Review*, the *New York Times* and even the *National Inquirer*. The reasons for the continuing delay in publication were many – more tragic than sinister. Rather than a 'Vatican conspiracy' or the unbridled arrogance of the original editors, it was mundane realities: lack of money and time, failure to recognize early on the magnitude and difficulty of the task, personal tragedies of alcoholism and illness. In December 1990, John Strugnell was removed from his position, and Emanuel Tov of the Hebrew University of Jerusalem appointed as editor-in-chief, along with Émile Puech of the École Biblique and Eugene Ulrich of the University of Notre Dame (who took primary responsibility for the biblical materials). Events came to a head in the fall of 1991, culminating in the announcement by the Israeli Antiquities Department in the Knesset on 27 October 1991 that the embargo on access to the scrolls and photographs had been lifted.

After the drama – and pathos – of this brief transformative period in 1990–91, the real work of getting the texts published could begin in earnest. For most scholars around the world, full accessibility came not with the events of 1991 but with the release in 1993 of a complete microfiche version of the negatives of the scrolls.[34] Now anyone with $900 and a good microfiche reader could have direct access to all of 6,269 plates of photos. Some of the anticipated perils of this new level of accessibility quickly became apparent when isolated but juicy tidbits (the so-called 'Crucified Messiah' text, for instance) found their way on to the front page of the *New York Times*, without benefit of either peer review or sober second thought. But, on the other hand, the assumption that everyone was eager to set to work to read new texts proved far too simplistic. As co-chair of the Qumran Section for the Society of Biblical Literature in those years, I was repeatedly cautioned that we would now be flooded with far more papers than we could possibly handle, as aspiring young scholars and an older generation that had been deprived of access for 40 years now eagerly turned to the task. This was not the case. The actual work of publishing a fragmentary text (and these were the only ones still left to be published) means technical skill in palaeography, familiarity with manuscripts, the tedium of searching down every single parallel from scratch, meticulous attention to detail, and the frustration of simply not having enough material to draw big conclusions – all these factors combined did not induce large numbers of people to devote months or years of their lives to a few damaged lines. The actual work of preparing editions remained in the hands of a rather small group of specialists. Emanuel Tov redivided and reassigned the remaining materials, and some 53 more scholars became involved in preparing one or more scrolls for publication in *DJD*.[35]

One of the distinctive features of this fifth decade was a series of major international scholarly conferences held at one or two-year intervals, beginning with the New York conference in honour of Yigael Yadin (1985), followed by commemorations of the fortieth anniversary of the discovery in Oxford (1987) and Haifa (1988), then Groningen (1989), Madrid (1991), Notre Dame (1993), Jerusalem (1994), Provo (1996), culminating with a massive conference in Jerusalem to mark the fiftieth anniversary (1997). An International Organization for Qumran Studies began meeting at three-year intervals (from 1992), and the newly established Orion Center for the Study of the Dead Sea Scrolls and Associated Literature at Hebrew University started holding an annual conference in 1996. The published volumes of papers given at these conferences are a major component of the Qumran bibliography of the decade. But beyond the printed page, these conferences served to create an international body of scholars bound by ties of collaborative work and personal friendship. Among the participants, new texts and theories often become common knowledge a couple of years before the printed version.

After a hiatus following the publication of *DJD* VII in 1982, the next volumes to appear finally were highly specialized and attracted the notice of few people other than textual critics: the Greek Minor Prophets Scroll from Nahal Hever (*DJD*

VIII, 1990) and a volume of Palaeo-Hebrew and Greek biblical manuscripts (*DJD* IX, 1992). Under Tov's editorship, volumes began to come fast and furiously by the second half of the fifth decade: the long-awaited 4QMMT (*DJD* X, 1994); biblical manuscripts, Genesis to Numbers (*DJD* XII, 1994), Deuteronomy to Kings (*DJD* XIV, 1995), Prophets (*DJD* XV, 1997); three volumes of parabiblical texts (*DJD* XIII, 1994; XIX, 1995; XXII, 1996); the cave 4 copies of the *Damascus Document* (*DJD* XVIII, 1996); and the first volume of wisdom texts (*DJD* XX, 1997). Suddenly scholars had a new problem – finding time to read all the texts available!

As the written texts became accessible, similar demands began to be heard for the publication of all the archaeological materials. In 1987, in conjunction with the centenary of their school, the École Biblique et Archéologique Français put together a team of scholars to prepare the definitive archaeological report on the work that had been done at Khirbet Qumran under Roland de Vaux in 1951–56: that is, all the artefacts (pottery, glass ware, coins, metal and stone ware and lamps), the written materials (some 70 short inscriptions on ostraca and graffiti), and the daily field records. The first volume appeared in 1994, and included some 538 photos from the 1950s plus a synthesis of de Vaux's field notes.[36] Renewed attention to archaeology has generated its own spate of theories, as diverse and contradictory as those based on the study of texts, and once again, when the total evidence is not yet available, theories can abound. Various proposals have been put forth to attempt to explain the nature of the settlement at Qumran: a luxurious villa (Donceel[37]), a Hasmonean residence subsequently converted into a cultic centre for the offering of sacrifices by the Essenes (Humbert[38]), even a commercial entrepot (Crown and Cansdale[39]). Many archaeologists (especially

Magness[40]) continue to defend and refine de Vaux's conclusion that the distinctive features (large buildings, extensive waterworks, walls) are best explained as the ruins of a communal sectarian settlement.

## The Sixth Decade: 1997–

After the excitement of the multiple fiftieth anniversary celebrations throughout 1997, attention turned to completing the publication of all the scrolls. As editor-in-chief, Emanuel Tov brought to the task superb organizational skill, expertise in the technical aspects of production and the ability to encourage – and sometimes pressure – editors to produce. Volumes continued to appear steadily: the liturgical texts (*DJD* XI, 1998; XXIX, 1999), the cave 11 materials that had been purchased by the Dutch Academy (*DJD* XXIII, 1998), the cave 4 copies of the *Rule of the Community* and related texts (*DJD* XXVI, 1998), the large wisdom instruction (*DJD* XXXIV, 1999), halakhic texts (*DJD* XXXV, 1999), texts written in cryptic script (*DJD* XXXVI, 2000), Psalms to Chronicles (*DJD* XVI, 2000), Aramaic texts (*DJD* XXXI, 2001), calendrical texts (*DJD* XXI, 2001), pseudo-prophetic texts (*DJD* XXX, 2001), and the inevitable miscellaneous volume (*DJD* XXXVIII, 2000). In addition, all the unidentified fragments were published (*DJD* XXXIII, 2001), most tiny pieces with only a few letters or partial letters, but since the volume appeared already at least a dozen fragments have been tentatively identified as belonging to some biblical or previously published work (often the identification has been made with the help of computer analysis to identify clusters of only two or three letters over a few lines).

# Fifty Years Plus: A Survey Decade by Decade

At the Society of Biblical Literature meeting in Denver, Colorado in 2001, the completion of the *DJD* series, inaugurated in 1955, was formally celebrated. As so often is the case in scrolls research, promise and reality did not quite match: two volumes had not appeared, one of Aramaic fragments (*DJD* XXXVII) and the long-awaited manuscripts of 1–2 Samuel (*DJD* XVII, published in 2005). We now have 11,594 pages of text and 1,312 plates of fragments.

It is to be hoped that the task of publishing the archaeological remains can likewise soon be brought successfully to a conclusion. A second volume in the archaeological series (2003) makes available all the ostraca and graffiti for the first time, plus a series of more technologically orientated studies on the pottery, carbon 14 dating, the textiles, ritual baths and pools, and metals.[41]

I leave the discussion of what might be expected in the rest of this decade for the final section (pp. 105–9), when we look ahead to the future of scrolls research.

## Notes

1. Memoirs were written by Mar Athanasius Yeshue Samuel, the Syrian Orthodox Archbishop of St Mark's monastery, *The Treasure of Qumran, My Story of the Dead Sea Scrolls*, and by John C. Trever, the young graduate student and amateur photographer in residence at the Albright Institute in 1947–48, *The Untold Story of Qumran*. Yigael Yadin included an account of how his father, Eleazer Sukenik, purchased a few of the scrolls from cave 1 in *The Message of the Scrolls*. For a lively, journalistic account of the early years, see Edmund Wilson, *The Dead Sea Scrolls, 1947–1969*.

2. For a brief survey, see the article 'Discovery and Purchase' in Lawrence H. Schiffmann and James C. VanderKam (eds), *Encyclopedia of the Dead Sea Scrolls*, pp. 208–12. Weston Fields, at the Dead Sea Scrolls Foundation, is currently writing a comprehensive account of the

early years that will draw on much previously unused archival material and will include interviews with many of the 'first generation' figures who are still living.

3. See further discussion in Chapter 2, pp. 40–8.

4. 1QS 7 13; *The Jewish War* 2.147.

5. The first sentence is from Albright's letter to John Trever, as reprinted in *The Untold Story of Qumran*, p. 85; the second sentence is from 'Notes from the president's desk', *BASOR* 110 (1948), 3.

6. Paul Bauchet, 'Transcription and Translation of a Psalm from Sukenik's Dead Sea scroll', *CBQ* 12 (1950), 331–5.

7. *The Treasure of the Hidden Scrolls of the Hebrew University* (1954, Hebrew; 1955, English, *The Dead Sea Scrolls of the Hebrew University*).

8. *The Dead Sea Scrolls of St. Mark's Monastery*, Volume 1: The Isaiah Manuscript and the *Habakkuk Commentary* (1950); Volume 2, fascicle 2: The *Manual of Discipline* (1951). Volume 2, fascicle 1 was reserved for the *Genesis Apocryphon* but never published. This badly damaged scroll was opened only with great difficulty, and eventually published by Nahman Avigad and Yigael Yadin in 1956, *A Genesis Apocryphon: A Scroll from the Wilderness of Judaea*.

9. Other caves at Wadi Murabba'at, Khirbet Mird and Nahal Hever were discovered in the search of the Judean wilderness. Although the materials from these caves are sometimes included in the general category 'Dead Sea Scrolls', I have not attempted to treat them in this book.

10. A few fragments were handed over to the Department of Antiquities only in the summer of 1958. For his reminiscences of these exciting days, see the interview with Frank Moore Cross by Herschel Shanks, *Frank Moore Cross: Conversations with a Bible Scholar*, p. 124.

11. Patrick Skehan, Jean Starcky and John Strugnell, 'Le travail d'édition des manuscrits de Qumrân,' *RB* 63 (1956), 49–67.

12. 'Out of the Desert', Religion Section of *Time*, Canadian edn (15 April 1957), p. 77.

13. For an account of the photography process, see John Strugnell, 'On the History of the Photographing of the Discoveries in the Judean Desert for the International Group of Editors' in *The Dead Sea Scrolls on Microfiche: Companion Volume*, pp. 123–34.

14. In the absence of a full archaeological report on the site, these lectures, published in a revised edition as *Archaeology and the Dead Sea*

*Scrolls*, have served as the prime source for de Vaux's work (until more recent publications, see note 37).

15. J. T. Milik, *Dix ans de découvertes dans le désert de Juda* (trans. John Strugnell, *Ten Years of Discovery in the Wilderness of Judea*); Frank Moore Cross, *The Ancient Library of Qumran and Modern Biblical Studies*, Haskell Lectures 1956–57.

16. Edited by Krister Stendahl, *The Scrolls and the New Testament*, 1957; reissued in 1992 with the same title.

17. According to the comprehensive bibliography compiled by Christoph Burchard, *Bibliographie zu den Handschriften von Toten Meer*, 1957.

18. For example, Maurice Baillet published an important collection of prayers, *The Words of the Luminaries*, already in a lengthy article in 1962, and John Strugnell made available the most significant sections of the *Songs of the Sabbath Sacrifice/The Angelic Liturgy* in a journal article in 1960.

19. The classic work that established the typology was an essay in 1965 by Frank Moore Cross, 'The Development of the Jewish Scripts' in *The Bible and the Ancient Near East: Essays in Honor of William Foxwell Albright*.

20. Many of these studies were subsequently collected in two important volumes, the first by Jerome Murphy O'Connor, *Paul and Qumran: Studies in New Testament Exegesis* and the second edited by James H. Charlesworth, *John and Qumran*.

21. Geza Vermes, 'The Impact of the Dead Sea Scrolls on Jewish Studies During the Last Twenty-five Years', *JJS* 26 (1975), 1–14.

22. This was not a formal publication in the *DJD* series but a monograph written by J. T. Milik in collaboration with Matthew Black, *The Books of Enoch: Aramaic Fragments of Qumran Cave 4*.

23. J. O'Callaghan published his work in Spanish, but it was quickly translated into English as 'New Testament Papyri in Qumrân Cave 7?' Supplement to *JBL* 91 (1972), 1–14.

24. For a recent attempt to revive the case, see Carsten Peter Thiede, *The Earliest Gospel Manuscript? The Qumran Papyrus 7Q5 and its Significance for New Testament Studies*.

25. Michael Knibb, 'Keeping up with Recent Studies: The Dead Sea Scrolls: Reflections on Some Recent Publications', *ET* 90 (1978–79), 294.

26. Norman Golb, 'The Problem of Origin and Identification of the

Dead Sea Scrolls', *PAPS* 124 (1980), 1–24.

27. Robert Eisenman, *Maccabees, Zadokites, Christians and Qumran*; Eisenman, *James the Just in the Habakkuk Pesher*.

28. For example, Eisenman's theory became known to the general public largely from the presentation of Michael Baigent and Richard Leigh in *The Dead Sea Scrolls Deception* and Neil Asher Silberman in *The Hidden Scrolls*.

29. The story of the recovery of the *Temple Scroll* has only gradually become public; see Yagael Yadin, 'The Temple Scroll – The Longest and Most Recently Discovered Dead Sea Scroll', *BAR* 10 (Sept–Oct, 1984), 32–49; H. Shanks, 'Intrigue and the Scroll: Behind the Scenes of Israel's Acquisition of the Temple Scroll', *BAR* 13 (Nov–Dec, 1987), 23–7. See the reminiscences of Frank Moore Cross in Shanks, *Conversations with a Bible Scholar*, pp. 135–42.

30. The issue of sectarian/non-sectarian is complex; for a perceptive and nuanced treatment, see the article of Carol Newsom, '"Sectually Explicit" Literature from Qumran' in *The Hebrew Bible and Its Interpreters*, pp. 167–87.

31. For example, the dissertations of Carol Newsom, *Songs of the Sabbath Sacrifice: A Critical Edition* (1985) and Eileen M. Schuller, *Non-Canonical Psalms from Qumran: A Pseudepigraphic Collection* (1986) were published in the Harvard Semitic Studies series.

32. The paper was eventually published in the conference volume, Elisha Qimron and John Strugnell, 'An Unpublished Halakhic Letter from Qumran' in *Biblical Archaeology Today: Proceedings of the International Congress on Biblical Archaeology Jerusalem, April 1984*, pp. 400–7.

33. Vermes, *The Dead Sea Scrolls: Qumran in Perspective*, p. 24.

34. *The Complete Dead Sea Scrolls Microfiche and Companion Volume*, prepared by Emanuel Tov, in conjunction with Stephen Pfann. In 1996 some 1,600 images were made available from the collection of John Allegro, *The Allegro Collection*, edited by George J. Brooke.

35. A complete list of *DJD* editors can be found in the final volume, *DJD* XXXIX, pp. 21–5.

36. The volume was prepared by Jean-Baptiste Humbert and Alain Chambon, *Fouilles de Khirbet Qumrân et de Aïn Feshkha*. In 2003 the section containing de Vaux's field notes was translated and revised by Stephen Pfann, *The Excavations of Khirbet Qumran and Aïn Feshkha*.

37. Robert Donceel and Pauline Donceel-Voûte, 'The Archaeology

of Khirbet Qumran' in Michael O. Wise et al. (eds), *Methods of Investigation of the Dead Sea Scrolls and the Khirbet Qumran Site*, pp. 1–38.

38. Jean-Baptiste Humbert, 'L'espace sacré a Qumrân: propositions pour l'archéologie', *RB* 101 (1994), 162–214.

39. Alan D. Crown and Lena Cansdale, 'Qumran: Was it an Essene Settlement?', *BAR* 20 (1994), 24–35, 73–8.

40. In *The Archaeology of Qumran and the Dead Sea Scrolls*, Jodi Magness has written the most comprehensive archaeological study that is possible at this time, given that many of the finds, including the pottery and glass ware, have not been published.

41. Jean-Baptiste Humbert and Alain Chambon, *Fouilles de Khirbet Qumrân et de Aïn Feshkha*, Volume II: Studies of Anthropology, Physics and Chemistry (2003).

# 2

# What Have We Learned About Scripture?

In the last chapter we looked at two of the earliest announcements about the Dead Sea Scrolls and the claim that this was a discovery with the potential to 'revolutionize our understanding' of both early Judaism and early Christianity. Now, over 50 years later, the language of revolution and new understanding is still being used when the discussion is focused specifically on the biblical scrolls. For instance, Eugene Ulrich, who has edited many of the copies of the books of the Hebrew Bible found at Qumran, began his lecture at the Jerusalem Conference in 1997: 'It is not too much to say that the two hundred biblical scrolls discovered at Qumran have revolutionized our understanding of the text of the Bible in antiquity.'[1] Similarly, at the Society of Biblical Literature fiftieth anniversary celebration, Devorah Dimant reminded us: 'One of the most striking changes brought about by the Qumran discovery is an entirely new understanding of the process by which the text of the Hebrew Bible took shape.'[2] And, in his comprehensive assessment once all of the biblical scrolls were published, Emanuel Tov came to the same conclusion: 'In many ways, the newly discovered texts have revolutionized the study of the text of the Hebrew Bible, as well as that of the Greek Bible.'[3]

## What Have We Learned About Scripture?

It is surprising to see the impact of the biblical scrolls in particular described in this way. In the 1950s when the first overviews were published listing what was contained in the new finds, many people were, in fact, disappointed to find that so many of the scrolls were copy after copy of books like Isaiah and Deuteronomy – after all, we already had these in our Bibles! Such scrolls seemed much less exciting than the discovery of previously unknown works like the *Book of the Giants*, or a 'brontologion' (manual for divination by thunder), or new collections of curses against your enemies. On the other hand, for both Christians and Jews with a primarily religious interest in the scrolls, these biblical manuscripts were often the most important part of the find – texts uncontaminated by generations of copyists, that would bring us closer to the 'original words' of the biblical writers and prophets. For some religious believers whose faith assured them that the Word of God had been passed down whole and entire, without error throughout the centuries, it was hoped that the scrolls could give scientific/objective proof of this accuracy of transmission. Others anticipated that the scrolls would resolve long-standing debates (especially questions at the centre of the conservative/liberal divide: Was there one Isaiah or three? Was the book of Daniel written at the time of the exile in the sixth century BC as genuine prophecy or was it written much later during the Maccabean revolt? Why the curious alternation of Hebrew and Aramaic in Daniel?). Still others were most interested in the practical implications: will we need to do redo our translations of the Bible into English and base them on the scrolls rather than the manuscripts which up to now had been used as the basis for translation? Over time it has become increasingly clear that while the scrolls might shed some light on such concerns, these are really not the key questions. Rather we ask – and are able to ask – new and different questions now because we have more information about the biblical text in the period prior to AD 70, data that was simply not known before. To some extent, we are still in the process of figuring out the right questions to ask.

The biblical scrolls comprise about one quarter of the manuscripts found at Qumran. There are approximately 200 biblical scrolls from Qumran itself, and at least another 20 or so scrolls if we include those from other caves and sites in the Judean desert (Murabba'at, Nahal Hever, Masada). This is a significant body of material, but it is important to be realistic about what has survived. In the first batch of scrolls recovered from cave 1 was the Isaiah Scroll, well preserved, virtually complete, over seven metres long, containing most of all 66 chapters of Isaiah. This scroll (or a facsimile thereof) is what people see on display at the Shrine of the Book in the Israel Museum, and it continues to shape popular perception of what a biblical scroll is like. In reality, however, most of the biblical scrolls, especially the 127 or so from cave 4, are very badly damaged; what has survived are small pieces, usually of a few partial lines, and the rest has been destroyed. Other than 1QIsa[a], there is only one other that has survived as a scroll with an extended series of consecutive (more or less complete) columns, the Psalms Scroll from cave 11 (if this is really a biblical Psalter! – see the discussion on pp. 47–8 below), and even this scroll is far from complete in that it contains only the final third of the psalms, beginning with Psalm 101. For many scrolls we may have only very small fragments, with a few lines and a few words (or even letters) in each line. Because the biblical text is already known, even tiny pieces can often be identified (sometimes with computer help) and then the original column reconstructed with more or less certainty – but the information that can be gleaned from such tiny bits is limited.

The publication of the biblical materials has taken a long time, in part precisely because of the difficulty of dealing with such fragmentary remains. When the International Team was formed in the 1950s, the fragments that could be identified on the initial reading as biblical were divided between Frank Moore Cross (of McCormick Theological College, and later Harvard University) and Monsignor Patrick Skehan (of Catholic University, Washington); some biblical texts in Greek recovered from other nearby caves went to the Dominican scholar, Dominique Barthélemy (and were eventually published by Emanuel Tov in *DJD* VIII).[4] When Skehan died, his material passed on to Eugene Ulrich (Notre Dame University) and Ulrich has now been the key figure in recent years in bringing the work on the biblical corpus to completion. Many of the larger and/or most interesting and significant pieces had already been published in dissertations or articles in the 1960s/1970s and thus have actually been part of the scholarly discussion for decades. Most of the *DJD* volumes of biblical materials were published between 1994 and 1997, except for the important volume with the books of Samuel (*DJD* XVII) which appeared in spring 2005.

## The Corpus of Biblical Manuscripts

When we make a list of the 200 or so biblical manuscripts, the list in itself is quite revealing.[5] There are over 80 copies of the books of the Pentateuch, over 50 copies of the prophets (including the copies of the book of Daniel in the count). The emphasis on Torah and prophets should not be surprising, for this community articulates its purpose and goal as: 'to seek God with a whole heart and soul, and do what is good and right before him as he commanded by the hand of Moses and all his servants the prophets' (1QS 1 2–3). Within the Law and the Prophets, three books predominate: there are 30 copies of Deuteronomy, 21 copies of Isaiah, and over 30 copies of the Psalms.[6] Deuteronomy is quoted or alluded to frequently in core sectarian texts, especially the *Rule of the Community*, and its covenant theology of reward and punishment was certainly fundamental to the sectarian worldview. Isaiah was a favourite prophet. His words 'prepare in the wilderness the way of the Lord; make straight in the desert a path for our God' (Isa. 40.3) are quoted to give the biblical justification for withdrawing (both geographically and metaphorically) to the wilderness for a life of study: 'This (way) is the study of the Law which he commanded by the hand of Moses, that they may do according to all that has been revealed from age to age and as the prophets have revealed by his Holy Spirit' (1QS 8 15–16). In addition, there are six copies of *pesher* (commentary) on Isaiah, more than on any other prophet. The Psalter too was read and studied as prophecy, and *pesharim* (commentaries) were written on it as on other prophetic books; how much the psalms were used for public, communal prayer and whether this influenced the number of copies is much more difficult to determine (see discussion on pp. 74–5 below). Hartmut Stegemann has even suggested that the preponderance of copies of Deuteronomy, Isaiah and Psalms may indicate that these books were the curriculum of study for those entering the community in their three years of initial formation. These are also the three books of the Hebrew Bible quoted or alluded to most frequently in the New Testament. If there were a functional 'canon within a canon' in Judaism in the first century, these books certainly formed the core.

Copies, often three or four or more, of all the other books of the Hebrew Bible were found in the caves, except for the book of Esther.[7] The 'omission' of Esther has occasioned much speculation: was it because this was a late, Persian-period book and the Qumran calendar does not mention the feast of Purim? Or was it because the book of Esther does not contain the name of God? Sometimes it has been suggested that a misogynist male celibate community simply did not like the one biblical book in which a woman is the heroine. But the reason for the absence of Esther may be much more mundane, basically a fluke; statistically it could be just by chance that no fragment has survived from such a short book (in comparison, from 1 and 2 Chronicles, which is many times longer than Esther, only one small fragment remains).

Finally, we should note that there are some copies, though few, of the biblical books in translation. There are five copies of four of the books of the Pentateuch (Exodus, Leviticus, Numbers and Deuteronomy) in Greek, plus the Greek scroll mentioned above of the Minor Prophets that was found at Nahal Hever. From cave 4 and cave 11 come two manuscripts that are a translation of the book of Job into Aramaic; there is also a small section of Leviticus in Aramaic (Lev. 16.1–15, 18–21), but it is hard to know if this is an Aramaic translation of the whole book or only an Aramaic version of this section dealing with the Day of Atonement that may have come from a ritual text. Given that the community wrote their own sectarian works in Hebrew, it is likely that everyone was expected to know Hebrew, so it is not obvious whether these translations served any functional purpose in worship or for study.

One of the more sensational claims – this one is revived regularly in the media particularly during the Christmas/Easter season – is that certain of the New Testament books can be found among the Greek fragments recovered from cave 7. It would indeed be news if copies of the gospels and even letters like 1 Timothy and 2 Peter (as has been proposed) were positively identified in the Qumran caves; not least of all, this would prove that these books were written prior to AD 68, much earlier than most New Testament scholars would date them. One fragment in particular, 7Q5, occasioned a great deal of media attention in 1972 when José O'Callaghan first proposed that it was actually a fragment of Mark 6.52–3, and this identification continues to be promoted by Carsten Thiede and a few others.[8] On the small papyrus fragment of five partial lines and about 20 letters or partial letters, there is no full word preserved (except for *kai*: 'and'); to fit what is preserved with the proposed Marcan text requires postulating a variant not found in any known copy of Mark 6 and a very problematic reading of certain other letters. The identification has not convinced most Qumran or New Testament scholars, and a much stronger case can be made that at least a number of the fragments in cave 7 are from a Greek translation of *Enoch*.

## What About the Differences?

The manuscripts found at Qumran give us copies of the biblical books that are approximately 1,000 years earlier than any copies that had been known previously. Prior to 1947, when scholars looked for the earliest copy of the Bible, they might be able to consult the fragmentary codex of some of the prophetic books from Cairo, dated AD 895, or the damaged Aleppo Codex of AD 925, but for a complete manuscript that contained all the biblical books it was necessary to use the Leningrad Codex, a large, beautifully handwritten codex (now preserved in Leningrad/St Petersburg); a colophon says that the scribe completed this work in AD 1008/1009. This is the manuscript that is typically used as the basis for printed Bibles in Hebrew (for example, the *Biblia Hebraica*) and the Hebrew text that forms the basis for translation into English and other languages. Now we have manuscripts from over 1,000 years earlier. A scholar studying Isaiah can now consult 1QIsa$^a$ from approximately 125 BC, and, for a few biblical books, manuscripts even considerably earlier (for example, 4QSam$^b$, dated about 225 BC). Even with this we do not, of course, have the 'original' words of Isaiah, and we still know very little about the process whereby his words were collected ('bind up the testimony, seal the teaching among my disciples' [Isa. 8.16]) and transmitted through the centuries. But the distance separating the oral preaching of the prophet and our earliest copy of his words is now less than 600 years, not some 1700 years. And in the case of a book like Daniel, the gap between composition and the written copies that we possess is only about a generation.

Given that we now have access to copies of the text of the Bible as it existed in the first centuries BC and AD, there is an obvious question: is this the same text as that found in the Leningrad Codex? The answer is both yes and no. When the Leningrad Codex and 1QIsa$^a$ (to take a concrete example) are compared, they are certainly similar: there was no wholesale rewriting nor large-scale additions, omissions or rewritings. In the Qumran copy Isaiah was a single book, with all 66 chapters. It is evident that the scribes who copied this book painstakingly by hand over the centuries copied with great care and accuracy. Religious Jews and Christians who had always been confident that the text they were studying had not been corrupted and changed as 'the Word of God' was transmitted through the ages could now point to the evidence of actual manuscripts.

But, in virtually any close comparison of even a few lines of text, differences will be found between the Leningrad Codex and the Qumran scroll – a different word, a different spelling, variation in order of words or verses, additions and omissions of a word or phrase. In letter-by-letter comparison of 1QIsa[a] and the Leningrad Codex, scholars have counted up hundreds of differences, thousands if we include every variation in spelling.[9] And if we look at 1QIsa[b], a second, more fragmentary copy of the book of Isaiah also found in cave 1, 1QIsa[b] is significantly different again from 1QIsa[a] – and in almost every case closer to the traditional Hebrew text found in the Leningrad Codex.

Text-critical scholars focus on places of differences and try to account for the variants; they seek to understand 'what is going on here in the text?' Sometimes a word/phrase that had long been recognized as problematic, even unintelligible, by both the rabbis and church fathers may suddenly become clear in the text found in a Qumran scroll. A classic and oft-quoted short example is a passage in Isaiah 21.8 where the prophet speaks of crying out and standing on the watchtower. In the midst of this rather ordinary passage, the Masoretic Text has the strange phrase 'and he cried, a lion'. Something seems wrong with a lion in this context. The Greek translators and some of the rabbis tried to make the word for 'lion' (*'arieh*) into a proper name; others added to the text so as to read 'he cried like a lion'; some suggested that the Hebrew text was in error and letters had been inverted in the process of copying because, with some slight rearrangement (remember that Hebrew at this time did not have vowels written in), the same letters could read 'the one who sees/a watchman' (*haro'eh*) and this fits well into the general context. When scholars looked at 1QIsaᵃ, they saw for the first time an actual Hebrew manuscript where the scribe had written *haro'eh*. This new information was quickly put to practical use. In 1948, Burrows carefully read and transcribed the entire 1QIsaᵃ manuscript on the boat from Israel to New York, and his copy was made available to the editorial committee that was working on the Revised Standard Version (RSV) translation into English. Here (as in 13 other places in Isaiah), the editorial committee chose to follow the Qumran text. Thus, in the RSV of Isaiah 21.8 we find, 'Then he who saw cried: upon a watchtower I stand, O Lord', rather than what had appeared heretofore in the King James Version: 'And he cried, A lion. My Lord, I stand upon the watchtower.'

In the years leading up to 1990 when the RSV was itself again being revised, the committee preparing the New Revised Standard Version (NRSV) had access to all scrolls – even those not yet officially published – because Eugene Ulrich was on the committee. They adopted more readings from the scrolls. Indeed for many people, one of the most concrete results of the Dead Sea Scrolls discovery was to find in their NRSV edition of the Bible a short paragraph at the end of 1 Samuel 10, after verse 27, verses that had not been in the Bible they had used previously. The narrative in this section of 1 Samuel had always raised questions, and commentators both ancient and modern suspected that something was missing. 1 Samuel 11 mentions a king Nahash of the Ammonites who wants to make a treaty on the condition that he be allowed to gouge out the eye of each person in the city – but there is no context or explanation for this strange request. 4QSam<sup>a</sup> has a couple of additional lines of text that sets this in a context of Nahash's acts of atrocity to the Gadites and Reubenites. The NRSV editors made a judgement that these verses had originally been part of the biblical narrative and had been lost in the process of copying (indeed, we can reconstruct how the eye of a scribe might easily have slipped from one word to another similar word, eliminating precisely this section), and thus the editors restored these verses in the NRSV translation from the 4QSam<sup>a</sup> manuscript.

In both these cases, and in thousands similar, the textual critic/translator is required to make a judgement. These are not mechanical decisions. We cannot simply assume that the earliest copy has the original text, because the Qumran scribe could be the one to introduce a copying error and the (much later) Leningrad Codex could have preserved the original. Especially in the second example above, the argument could be made – and has been – the other way, namely, that these verses were added secondarily by a scribe at some stage in the process of transmission who saw the very same problem we do and inserted these words of explanation; if this is the case, then as a secondary addition, should these words be included in a modern translation.

But there is still more. When scholars worked through manuscript after manuscript from the caves in the 1960s and drew up detailed lists of all the places where each differed from the text they found in their printed *Biblia Hebraica*, it soon became apparent that more was at stake than the random mistakes of individual scribes. Different scrolls corresponded, more or less closely, with variations that scholars had long recognized existed between three different versions of the biblical text already known. The text found in the Leningrad Codex was the traditional Hebrew text that had been used by the rabbis and scribes since the second century AD, the so-called Masoretic Text (MT). When the Bible was translated into Greek sometime around 200 BC (the Septuagint or LXX), the translators of some books clearly had before them a somewhat different text, but since we only have the Greek, in practice it is often very difficult to decide whether a specific difference stemmed from a different base text or whether the change had been introduced by the translator. Most of the differences are, again, small and minor, but occasionally there can be significant variation (for example, the LXX of the book of Jeremiah is about one-seventh shorter than the MT, with hundreds of verses not included). The Samaritan Pentateuch (the first five books of the Bible as they were handed down among the Samaritans) witnessed yet another form of the text, often somewhat longer and more expansive than the MT.

When the copies of the biblical scrolls were examined as a whole, it soon became obvious that some corresponded basically to the form of the text that would eventually become the Masoretic Text; others were closer to the text as underlies the Septuagint; still others had features characteristic of the Samaritan Pentateuch, and a certain number showed no consistent alignment with any of the three. Clearly, in the first century BC and on into the first half of the first century AD, the biblical text was not yet totally fixed; different textual versions existed, all being copied and in use at Qumran and throughout Palestine. Various theories have been proposed to try to account for this situation: Frank Moore Cross, following ideas already sketched out by his teacher W. F. Albright in the very early years when he was first studying the biblical scrolls, proposed that 'local texts' had developed geographic-ally, in Babylon (proto-Masoretic), Egypt (Septuagint) and Palestine (Samaritan). Other scholars see the differences as reflecting different literary editions, socio-religious distinc-tions, or multiple variants.[10]

Clearly the community at Qumran was able to live with such textual diversity and plurality. It was only slightly later that a single fixed Hebrew text came to be adopted. We know virtually nothing about the process, only the final result; that is, biblical scrolls found at Murrabba'at or Masada (from the end of the first century AD) are all basically the same. The MT became the traditional text for the Jewish community until today. The LXX was 'the Bible' for Christians at least up until the Renaissance/Reformation, when the Christian churches became more concerned to read the Old Testament in the original Hebrew, and then they too followed the MT. For the most part, the Samaritan Pentateuch was known and used only by that small community through the ages.

The implications of all this are more significant for some books of the Hebrew bible than for others. For instance, the text of Genesis is quite similar in all copies and versions. But for the book of Jeremiah, as we have noted, the MT and the LXX are very different. At Qumran we find copies of both, the long form like that of the MT (4QJer[a, c]) and the short form, about 13 per cent shorter (4QJer[b, d]). We can now be certain that the short form of Jeremiah actually existed in Hebrew and was not just an abbreviation made by the Greek transla-tors. All this has major implications for how we understand the process of the compilation and editing of the book of Jeremiah, and commentators on Jeremiah now need to work with both the long and the short versions. Not only for Jeremiah but more broadly, these Hebrew scrolls have had the unexpected result of sparking a real revival in the serious study of the LXX.

To give just one more example of a biblical book where the Qumran materials have generated major rethinking, we can turn to the book of Psalms. As we have already noted, there are many copies of the psalms, but the manuscript evidence is very complex to interpret (for instance, when we have only small fragments, as in the case with many psalm scrolls, it is difficult to know the order of the psalms unless the end of one and the beginning of another has been preserved). The question is: was the content of the Psalter and the order of the psalms fixed relatively early (perhaps already by the third century BC), or was the content and order still fluid on into the first century AD, so that different versions of the Psalter were being used in the community at Qumran? There is general agreement that the first part of the Psalter, Psalms 1–89, had been stabilized first; all the copies that we find at Qumran seem to agree with the MT in this section. The problem comes with the latter part. Some manuscripts at Qumran do seem to have the same order and content as the MT throughout. But we also have the large and beautifully written scroll (on ibex skin) from cave 11, 11QPs[a], which contains 41 psalms beginning with Psalm 101. The order of the psalms in 11QPs[a] is different than in the MT (for example Psalms 101, 102, 103, 109, 105, 146, 148, 121 and so on), and other compositions are interspersed: a wisdom poem that appears also in Sira 51; the Words of David from 2 Samuel 23; two psalms that had been known previously only in translation in Syriac Psalters (Pss 154, 155), Psalm 151 that is included in the Septuagint Psalter, and three previously unattested psalms (A Plea for Deliverance, The Apostrophe to Zion, The Hymn to the Creator). Towards the end of the scroll there is a prose passage listing all the songs of David which 'he spoke through prophecy which was given him from before the Most High' (11QPs$^a$ 27 2–11). The question is whether 11QPs$^a$ is a 'real' Psalter, that is, an alternative collection to the MT?[11] Or, was this some type of secondary compilation of diverse materials, perhaps put together for liturgical purposes or as an early example of a 'prayer book'? If the first option is correct, the make-up of the Psalter was still not fixed even as late as the first century AD; if we go with the second, 11QPs$^a$ is a completely different type of document and can be removed from discussions of the biblical scrolls. There is a lively debate, ongoing among scholars, over precisely this question, and at this point it is not clear that we have enough evidence to make a firm decision.

### What was 'the Bible' at Qumran?

Throughout this chapter we have been talking rather glibly about 'the Bible' and 'biblical scrolls'. But these expressions are much more problematic than they may seem at first glance. Recently, Eugene Ulrich began an article with the deliberately provocative statement: 'The first statement we should make about the Bible at Qumran is that we should probably not think of a "Bible" in first century BC or the first century AD, at Qumran or elsewhere.'[12]

Ulrich is not claiming that the Jews had no authoritative and sacred books. By this time, the five books of Moses and the words of the prophets clearly had a special status, and there seems to have been some third, less well defined category. This is simply assumed in texts such as 4QMMT C 9–10, 'we [have written] to you that you may have understanding in the book of Moses [and in the words of the pro]phets and in Davi[d]'; and Luke 24.27: 'Then beginning with Moses and the prophets, he interpreted to them the things about himself in the scriptures.' But if we wanted to print up 'the Bible' that was used by the people of Qumran, we would quickly find ourselves faced with a host of unanswerable questions.[13] Which book of Jeremiah should we include – the long or the short one? Should 11QPs[a] be included? What about Ben Sira and Tobit (books that were not included in the Bibles of the rabbis but were included in the LXX)? Do we include books like *Enoch* or *Jubilees*? These seem to have been very significant, even simply based on the number of copies preserved (over 20 copies of *Enoch* and 15 or 16 of *Jubilees* – many more copies than of books like Judges or Chronicles or Ecclesiastes). If usage is a criterion, the *Damascus Document* (CD 16 2–4) quotes *Jubilees* as an authoritative source for the determination of times, much in the same way that the Epistle of Jude (v. 14) quotes *1 Enoch* 1.9 as a prophetic word that all would recognize and accept. So what status did these books have? And in printing a 'Qumran Bible', how would we arrange it – do we put Daniel with the Prophets (as in the LXX) or with the Writings (as in the MT)?

It is probably anachronistic and basically unhelpful even to pose the question in quite this way. We cannot transpose our present understanding of a canon – a fixed list of books in a certain order – back to the first century when such a canon did not exist. What the scrolls have given us is a window into a period of fluidity, when the boundaries of inclusion/exclusion had not yet been clearly marked out, when this community may have included as authoritative certain books that were not accepted by other Jews and later rabbinic tradition. But it is precisely because of our greater appreciation of the variation and diversity that did exist prior to AD 70 that scholars have been led to reconsider why and how the process of consolidation took place in the decades immediately after the destruction of the temple. Questions of 'What is in the Bible?' 'Who decides?' 'Why does it matter?' are being asked now more pointedly than at any time since the era of the Reformation – without the simplistic presupposition that fuelled so much of the earlier debate that we can readily recover 'the Bible of Jesus'. Probably few of the first generation of scrolls scholars would have guessed that these manuscripts would revolutionize our thinking and lead us, 50 years later, to ponder anew so many fundamental questions about the development of what we call 'the Bible'.

## Notes

1. Eugene Ulrich, 'The Qumran Scrolls and the Biblical Text' in Lawrence H. Schiffman, Emanuel Tov and James C. VanderKam (eds), *The Dead Sea Scrolls Fifty Years After Their Discovery 1947–1997*, p. 51.

2. Devorah Dimant, 'The Scrolls and the Study of Early Judaism' in Robert A. Kugler and Eileen M. Schuller (eds), *The Dead Sea Scrolls at Fifty: Proceedings of the 1997 Society of Biblical Literature Qumran Section Meetings*, p. 47.

3. Emanuel Tov, 'The Biblical Texts from the Judean Desert – An Overview and Analysis of the Published Texts' in Edward D. Herbert and Emanuel Tov (eds), *The Bible as Book: The Hebrew Bible and the Judaean Desert Discoveries*, p. 139.

4. These fragments were purchased from the Bedouin in 1952–54, who said that they had been found in Wadi Seiyal (hence they were called the Wadi Seiyal collection). Further excavations have established that at least some of them, including the important scroll of the Minor Prophets in Greek, actually came from caves in Nahal Hever (which is how they are now designated).

5. It is difficult to give an absolute number of biblical scrolls. The number will vary depending on what we consider 'biblical', that is, part of an accepted canon of Scripture (see discussion pp. 48–50 below); for example, whether copies of Ben Sira and Tobit are included in the count. Sometimes when we have just a few fragments it is not clear if the scroll contained only a sub-section/excerpted passage or the whole biblical book (for instance, only fragments of Psalm 119 are preserved from 4QPs[b, h]; are these copies of just this psalm or of the whole Psalter?).

6. Above all with the Psalms, it is difficult to determine what is a 'biblical Psalter' and what is another type of collection (see discussion pp. 47–8 below), or a copy of only a sub-section of the collection.

7. It could be said that there is also no copy of Nehemiah. However, Ezra/Nehemiah seem to have been considered as a single book at this time, and there are three fragments of Ezra (4Q117).

8. See p. 19 and the bibliography in notes 23 and 24 of Chapter 1.

9. Hebrew orthography allows for different spellings of the same word, depending on whether certain letters are inserted to indicate vowels ('full' orthography) or whether the word is written without these vowels. Such variation in spelling is commonplace in both biblical Hebrew and Modern Hebrew, even within the same passage.

10. Eugene Ulrich has developed the idea of literary editions; Shemaryahu Talmon focuses on socio-religious differences; and Emanuel Tov has eschewed the explanation of three textual families in favour of emphasizing a number of textual forms. Much of the scholarly writing on these theories is very technical, but for a short, clear explanation, see the section on 'The Scrolls and the Text of the Hebrew Bible/Old Testament' in James C. VanderKam and Peter W. Flint, *The Meaning of the Dead Sea Scrolls*, pp. 140–5.

11. Two other manuscripts, 11QPs[b] and 4QPs[e], seem to have the same order and contents as 11QPs[a]; that is, 11QPs[a] is not just a 'one-time' maverick copy.

12. Eugene Ulrich, 'The Bible in the Making: The Scriptures Found at Qumran' in Peter W. Flint (ed.), *The Bible at Qumran: Text, Shape and Interpretation*, p. 51. In light of Ulrich's hesitation, I have entitled this chapter, 'What Have We Learned About Scripture?' rather than 'What Have We Learned About the Bible?' But to eliminate the language of 'Bible/biblical' totally became so convoluted in practice that I ended up going back to the standard terminology in the chapter itself.

13. Martin Abegg, Peter Flint and Eugene Ulrich have attempted to do precisely this in publishing *The Dead Sea Scrolls Bible*. They have tended to opt for inclusivity, including books such as Ben Sira, Tobit, *Jubilees* and *Enoch* as well as 11QPs[a].

# 3

# What Have We Learned About Prayer and Worship?

I will make bold to approach the topic of prayer and worship from a more autobiographical perspective. The editing of some of the prayers and psalms in the Dead Sea Scrolls has been my own area of work over the last 20-plus years, and perhaps my experience can serve to illustrate how scholars more broadly have come to appreciate the significance and richness of this type of material.

When I was about to embark on doctoral studies in 1977, I knew that I wanted to focus on post-exilic Judaism, the area of Second Temple Judaism that was just becoming a field of study in its own right. I had been working for a few years at the pastoral level (particularly in the area of church music) in implementing the liturgical reforms of Vatican II in the Catholic Church, and I was interested in Jewish–Christian relations – and somehow, I wanted to bring this all together in. my graduate studies. With all the naivety of a beginning doctoral student, I outlined my plans for writing a thesis that would uncover the Jewish roots of Christian liturgy by comparing early Christian prayers with Jewish prayers to show mutual influences and developments. When I got to Harvard, my supervisor, John Strugnell, gently pointed out that perhaps such a grand synthesis was somewhat premature, or at best could only be highly speculative. First of all, what was I going to compare? Our earliest copies of the Jewish prayerbook (Siddur) came from the eighth or ninth centuries AD (for example, the Siddur of Rab Amran Gaon), and we needed to know what Jews said many centuries earlier when they prayed in order to have any firm grounds of comparison. But Strugnell was able to offer me a way to move forward: there *was* in fact material that would enable me to pursue some of these very questions. As a member of the International Team of scholars editing the Dead Sea Scrolls, he had in his allotment a number of unpublished manuscripts with Jewish prayers and psalms that were contemporary with the beginnings of Christianity. Strugnell suggested that I might make a much better contribution to scholarship by concentrating the next years of my life on a few specific fragments, trying to read the letters on the dark and torn pieces, translating them for the first time, and puzzling out what sort of texts these might be. And so I began a fascinating study, some 20-plus years of working on and thinking about this type of material.

### 4Q380 and 4Q381: Non-canonical Psalms

I began by preparing a first edition of two unpublished manuscripts, 4Q380 and 4Q381.[1] There were some 97 pieces in all, the largest consisting of 16 partial lines, the smallest containing only two or three letters. This was clearly a collection of psalms, not the 150 psalms we know from the Hebrew Bible, but poetic compositions that we had never seen before. The two manuscripts contain very similar psalm-like compositions, but there is no overlapping text, so it is difficult to be certain if we have two copies of the same collection or two different collections. Like the biblical psalms, these poems are written in concise, balanced parallel lines. They express sentiments of praise, confession of sin and petition for God's help, and treat standard themes like creation (4Q381 1) and the praise of Zion (4Q380 1). Like the biblical psalms, many of them begin with a title: 'Prayer of Manasseh, king of Judah, when the King of Assyria put him in prison' (4Q381 33 8); 'Psalm of the Man of God' (4Q381 24 4). In one fragment the right-hand side of the column is missing just where the name of the speaker would have appeared: '[Prayer of . . .] king of Judah: Listen, my God . . .' (4Q381 31 4); since the psalm laments 'the days of my existence are stored up, what can a weak man do,' perhaps it was Hezekiah, who prayed a psalm when he was ill (Isa. 38). Another fragment begins with the words, 'Psalm of [ ,' and breaks off right there (4Q380 4). There is a 'Psalm of Obadiah' (4Q380 1 ii 8); one might wonder why a minor prophet like Obadiah is credited with writing a psalm, and all that remains of his composition is the single phrase, 'truth in it and his loving-kindness'.

Both manuscripts had been copied in approximately 75 BC, but when were they composed and by whom? In the 1980s, when I was preparing the first edition, there was still a predisposition to assume that all the materials found in the caves were written by the specific community that lived at Qumran, whether we identify these people specifically as the Essenes or not. But these psalms did not have the particular vocabulary and theology or world outlook of the *Rule of the Community*, *War Scroll* or the *Thanksgiving Psalms* that we knew from cave 1. There was no language of 'sons of light/sons of darkness', no dualistic contrast of light versus darkness, good versus evil. In poetic style, these compositions are closer to the biblical psalms than to the *Thanksgiving Psalms*. As we have just seen, they are attributed not to a contemporary figure like the Teacher of Righteousness, but pseudepigraphically to biblical characters of old. The name used for God is the Tetragrammaton (*yhwh*), a term carefully avoided in sectarian compositions in favour of *'el* ('God') – even when quoting from a biblical verse with the divine name, it is paraphrased or some substitution is used. Thus, I made the argument that these poems were composed two or three centuries earlier, in the fourth or third, maybe early second century BC. It is only because they were used, or at least a copy was included in the collection of manuscripts at Qumran, that they have come down to us. This suggests that there may have been many psalms composed in Persian and Hellenistic times but that only a portion has been preserved in the collection of the Hebrew Bible, and now some more can be recovered as part of the library of Qumran.

## The Corpus of Psalms and Prayers from Qumran

Psalms and prayers were found already among the manuscripts from cave 1.[2] Most significant was the scroll purchased by Eleazer Sukenik from the antiquities dealer Kando, which he published in 1954/55 under the title *Thanksgiving Scroll*. This is a collection of approximately 30 religious poems (the exact number was hard to determine since the scroll is badly damaged, and Sukenik, in an effort to make this new material available quickly, did not attempt to reconstruct how the four sheets and 66 small fragments fit together). These poems are clearly modelled on the biblical thanksgiving genre. They have a standard beginning, 'I give thanks to you' or 'Blessed are you', and then go on to outline what God has done for the psalmist: delivered him from his enemies, given him knowledge, brought him into the *yahad* (the community, the same word as in the *Rule of the Community*). In one group of psalms, the speaker seems to be a leader, one to whom God has granted special revelation with which he is to instruct others: 'You have manifested your might through me; you have revealed yourself to me in your power as perfect light . . . all those who are gathered in your covenant inquire of me' (1QH[a] 12 24).[3] Many scholars think that these psalms may have been written by the founder, the Teacher of Righteousness. Other compositions are more general, and express both a profound sense of human sinfulness and praise for God's grace: 'I have beheld your marvels [towards the children of] grace and I know that righteousness is yours, and in your mercies there is [hope for me] but without your grace [destruction] without end' (1QH[a] 19 19). The existence of this type of composition makes a profound statement about the community that stands behind the scrolls. These were Jews who were concerned not only with the correct interpretation of the law and grandiose speculation about the imminent 'end of days' and the final battle; a rich devotional piety shaped their daily life as they turned to God to offer praise and thanksgiving.

There was a second copy, very fragmentary, of the *Thanksgiving Psalms* (1QH[b]), recovered by the archaeologists from among the fragments left behind in cave 1; indeed, this is the only sectarian document of which two copies were preserved in cave 1, and this fact in itself reinforces the importance of this collection.[4] Also in the *War Scroll* from cave 1, in addition to elaborate plans for every detail of the arrangement of the troops and the conduct of battle, there is a lengthy section that gives the texts of the hymns and prayers to be said by the priests and high priests (1QM 10–15, 17–19). Some of these are perhaps victory hymns from the Maccabean period, slightly re-edited, and ready to be used at the last days. Another document, the *Rule of Blessings* (1QSb), attached to the *Rule of the Community* in the cave 1 manuscript, contains a long series of blessings that are to be recited by the *Maskil* (the Instructor), to bless the members of the community, the priests and the messiah. The mention of the messiah suggests that this is another text ready to be used at the end-times, though the blessings may have been pronounced proleptically in the present era, perhaps at the meals of the community where the coming of the messiah was anticipated (see 1QSa 2 10–22). Also from cave 1 is the *Genesis Apocryphon*, which retells in Aramaic the stories of Genesis with expansions, including the addition of prayers. For example, when Abraham's wife Sarah was taken by the king of Egypt, the biblical text says little about how Abraham responded; in the *Genesis Apocryphon*, Abraham is presented explicitly as a man of prayer, and his actual words are included: 'That night I prayed and I begged and I implored, and I said in my sorrow while my tears ran down, "Blessed are you, O Most High God, Lord of all worlds"' (1QapGen 20 12–13).

Thus, from the very early years of Qumran research, scholars knew that prayers and psalms were one of the genres found in the scrolls. However, this type of material initially attracted less scholarly interest than the laws and community rules, and certainly less media attention than some sensational little fragments about the messiah or the end of days. Those scrolls, most very fragmentary, containing prayers and psalms were published slowly over the next 20 years, often first in preliminary articles, then in *DJD* VII (1982) and two volumes devoted to liturgical texts (*DJD* XI, 1998; *DJD* XXIX, 1999), plus various miscellaneous pieces (*DJD* XXXVII, 2000). In the early 1990s, Esther Chazon counted a total of over 200 different prayers;[5] the exact number is not so important (the count can be done in different ways) but what is established is that we now have a significant corpus of previously unknown materials for study. Because so many important texts have been published recently, in this area of study above all, scholars are still exploring how we should put all this together and even what questions should be asked. The first full book-length study of the prayers and hymns did not appear until 1994 and there is still much more work to be done.[6]

In addition to the actual texts of prayers and psalms, there are expository statements about praying, and regulations about how and when to pray. Let us begin with these.

### The Practice of Prayer

One thing that is distinctive is that the community of Qumran put their prayers into written form. This was in marked contrast to the practice of subsequent centuries in rabbinic Judaism which discouraged the setting down of prayers in writing (*t. Shabb.* 13.4). One of the difficulties in studying Jewish prayer (particularly as it developed after the destruction of the temple in AD 70) is that although there are scattered references, and occasionally even the actual words of blessings in the Mishnah and in the Talmuds, prayer was basically oral. As mentioned earlier, the earliest preserved copies of the Siddur are dated only to the ninth century. The scrolls fill in a stage in the development of Jewish prayer-forms that previously had been without written texts.

Although I would not want to press this too hard, perhaps prayers were written down by the Essenes precisely because the recitation of prayers played such a central role in their lives. This group of Jews made the radical claim that prayer (in conjunction with a way of life lived strictly according to Torah as properly interpreted) was like the sacrifices of the temple, and therefore prayer could function in its own right as a means of making atonement. The language of the cult, the temple and its sacrifices, was applied to prayer:

> In order to atone for the guilt of iniquity and for the unfaithfulness of sin, and for approval for the earth, without the flesh of burnt offerings and without the fats of sacrifice – the offering of the lips in compliance with the decree will be like the pleasant aroma of justice and the perfectness of behaviour will be acceptable like a free-will offering. (1QS 9 4–5)

This understanding that prayer itself was worship (*avodah*) and could serve as a means of atonement may have developed as a pragmatic response to a perceived crisis. This community made the accusation that the sacrifices in the present Jerusalem temple under the existing priesthood were being carried out according to wrong halakhic practice (as spelled out in 4QMMT) and, even more seriously, according to the wrong calendar (a lunar calendar rather than the solar calendar). Thus they determined that while they could not take part in the regular fixed daily, Sabbath and festival sacrifices, their life of prayer and Torah observance could accomplish the same goal of establishing a right relationship with God. This was not an anti-temple, anti-sacrifice stance per se. In looking ahead to the final days of the great battle of the Sons of Light against the Sons of Darkness, the first stage of victory after seven years would involve the restoration of temple worship in Jerusalem (1QM 2 1–6). That is, prayer was not meant to replace ultimately the sacrificial system that had been ordained by God for all eternity and revealed in the Torah; only in the present 'time of Belial' did it need to take on that role. The claim that it was possible to live a life of holiness apart from the temple system was a radical one and raised the same issues that would have to be dealt with within the rest of Judaism after the destruction of the Temple in AD 70, and also by the early Christian church (as discussed especially in the Epistle to the Hebrews).

When the scrolls talk of prayer, it is prayer as a corporate activity. The *Rule of the Community* stipulates that 'they shall eat together, they shall bless together, and they shall take counsel together' (1QS 6 2–3). 'The Many' are to come together one third of each night 'to read the book, to explain the regulation and to bless together' (1QS 6 7–8). Prayers are formulated in the first person plural, and there are some hints of a dialogical or antiphonal style, as for example the common response of 'amen, amen'. There must have also been personal words of devotion and petition, the spontaneous turning to God in times of crisis or of joy, but prayers of this type have not been preserved.

What would the prayer life of this community have involved? Much is speculation: we have bits and pieces, but we do not have a daily prayer book or the type of ritual books that later outline the liturgical life of Christian monasteries. There is some evidence for set fixed times of prayers: 'with the offering of the lips he will bless him (God) during the set times that he prescribed' (1QS 10 1, also 1QH$^a$ 20 7–14). These times are set in accordance with the order of the cosmos: the regular cycle of morning and evening, the beginnings of the months, the festivals, the sabbatical years, and jubilee years (1QS 10 1b–8). It is through prayer that the community is brought into harmony with the whole of the cosmos and with the angelic world, whose inhabitants also praise God according to the cosmic order (as expressed in the *Hymn to the Creator*, 'Separating light from darkness, by the knowledge of his mind he established the dawn. When all his angels had witnessed it, they sang aloud' [11QPs$^a$ 26 11–12]). In addition to prayers recited at sunrise and sunset (we will look at some concrete examples in a moment), there was a communal meal, which according to Josephus (*The Jewish War* 2.129–33) was held at noon and, in a modified form, in the evening. These regular meals were in some sense a religious act: bathing and purity was required to participate in the meal; there was an order and hierarchy in the seating arrangements; the meal (or at least parts of it) was restricted to those who had undergone the full time of formation and testing and were fully initiated members of the group (1QS 6 16–23); a priest had to be present and he had the prerogative to say the blessings; in fact, in the last days when both the Messiah of David and the Priest are present at the meal, it is the latter who will have precedence in pronouncing the blessing (1QSa 2 17–23). Josephus refers to the blessings that were said at meals ('at the beginning and at the end they bless God as the Giver of life' [*The Jewish War* 2.131]), but no actual text of these blessings is preserved in the scrolls. According to the passage from 1QS quoted earlier, there was in addition some type of gathering held every night (or perhaps every third night of the year) which combined blessing, deliberation and study of the sacred texts.

Where did people pray? Those living in various towns and

cities presumably found places to gather for prayer, but there are no archaeological sites that we can recognize as places of prayer. Since the basic unit was an assembly of ten (1QS 6 3, 6) we need not think in terms of a large public building used only for this purpose; like the early Christians, they could have gathered in private homes. There is one passage in the *Damascus Document* – the interpretation has been much disputed – that discusses regulations for 'everyone who enters a house of prostration' (CD 11 21–2): there is to be purification by washing before entering, and the blowing of trumpets. This sounds like a reference to the temple (where people prostrated), but it has been argued recently that 'the house of prostration' was the Essene term for their local centres for worship.[7] If this is the case, it suggests that Essene worship incorporated features of temple worship, (prostrations, ritual purification before entrance and blowing of the trumpets) in quite a different way than what was done in the synagogue. The public synagogue was a place of gathering for the reading and exposition of the Torah; recall that when Jesus goes into the synagogue at Nazareth he reads from the scroll of Isaiah and expounds on the text (Luke 4.16–22); there is no explicit mention of reciting prayers. How much a set prayer structure was part of synagogue worship in the decades prior to AD 70 is a matter of ongoing dispute in the study of the development of the synagogue service.

## Morning and Evening and Sabbath Prayers

Let us now look at a few specific prayer texts as selected examples, beginning with prayer at sunrise (dawn) and sunset (late afternoon/evening). As noted above, these times of cosmic change, from light to darkness and back again, are of special importance. Josephus says of the Essenes: 'Before sunrise they speak no profane word but recite certain ancestral prayers to/towards the sun as though entreating it to rise' (*The Jewish War* 2.128). The hymn-like text at the end of the *Rule of the Community* expresses this more poetically: 'At the beginning of the dominion of light in its time, and at its end when it retires to its appointed place . . . when the heavenly lights shine out from the dwelling place of holiness, and also when they retire to the place of glory' (1QS 10 1–3). The text continues: 'With the coming of day and night I will enter the covenant of God, and when evening and morning depart, I will recite his decrees' (1QS 10 10); this probably alludes to the recitation of the *Shema*: 'Hear, O Israel, the LORD your God is one' (Deut. 6.4). In later tradition, this recitation is understood as the taking on of God's covenant, and is to be repeated 'when you lie down and when you rise'. The claim, 'I will recite his decrees' may refer the recitation of the Ten Commandments; there is some evidence that the Decalogue was included in the synagogue service at an early stage, even though it was later removed. The psalmist says, 'I will bless his name' (1QS 10 13); sometimes this is taken as evidence that actual blessings were already fixed for before and after the *Shema*, as later became standard in the daily liturgy, but perhaps this is reading too much into a more general phrase.

There are two collections of short prose prayers that are associated with morning and evening. The *Daily Prayers* (4Q503), preserved in only one copy, is a collection of blessings for each day of one month. The scroll is very damaged, with some 225 small fragments. No prayer is preserved complete, but because they are so formulaic we can reconstruct much of the regular structure. There is a standard rubrical-type notation for the evening: 'On the x-day of the month in the evening, they shall bless and answer and say . . .'; and for the morning: 'When the sun goes forth to illumine the earth they shall bless and answer and say . . .' Each prayer begins with a distinctive blessing (*baruk*) formula in the third person: 'Blessed be the God of Israel who did xxx,' and the prayer sometimes concludes with a blessing in the second person, 'Blessed be you/your name, O God of Israel'. Then someone (perhaps the priest) addresses the congregation directly with the words, 'Peace be upon you, Israel' (cf. Pss 125.5, 128.6).

Two features of these prayers are of special significance for what they tell us about how Jewish prayer developed. The prayer begins: 'Blessed be the God of Israel'. In the standard Jewish prayer book, the basic formula is that of the blessing: *baruk 'atta 'adonai 'elohenu melek ha'olam* – Blessed are you, O Lord our God, king of the universe. The *Daily Prayers* (along with others with similar formula) give evidence that this way of structuring prayer was becoming a set pattern already in the first century BC. It was, however, not yet as standardized and fixed as in subsequent centuries and there is considerably more variation in the formulary patterns in the scrolls than in later liturgy.[8] A second distinctive feature are phrases that talk of the joining of the prayers on earth with the prayers of the angels in heaven: 'we with the holy ones . . . those praising with us'. If one is to 'pray with the angels', then it is easy to see why the issue of the correct calendar is absolutely critical: if the earthly community is celebrating a feast on a given day and the heavenly angels are on a different calendar, there is a problem! Prayer with the angels is an important element in statutory Jewish prayer as it developed until today; in every service the words of the heavenly seraphim from Isaiah 6, 'Holy, holy, holy is the Lord of hosts', appear at least twice. Among liturgical scholars there has been a long-standing dispute as to whether the use of this *Qedushah* (the triple Holy) was an early or a late (perhaps even medieval) development, and whether it may have begun with Sabbath prayer and was only subsequently extended to weekdays, perhaps under the influence of mystical, kabbalistic circles. These were very difficult questions to answer when the only evidence we had were medieval prayer books from the tenth century and later. Now 4Q503 shows us that praying with the angels was a very early motif that was already part of prayer before the destruction of the temple – and on weekdays, not just on the Sabbath.

There is another set of prayers that may also have been said twice each day, morning and evening, though this is less certain. The title of the work, *The Words of the Luminaries*, was written on the outside of one copy (4Q504). This is a collection of prayers for each day of the week. 4Q504 is very damaged, but the original shape of the scroll was reconstructed by Esther Chazon in her dissertation at Hebrew University. These prayers follow a set structure and the series must have been written as a literary whole. Again there is a rubrical title, for example, for Wednesday, 'Prayer for the fourth day'. Each prayer seems to begin in the same way, not with a blessing but with an imperative: 'Remember, O Lord'. This is followed by an extended historical narrative that is divided over the consecutive days of the week from the creation of Adam (Sunday), through a retelling of the events of Exodus and the giving of the law, to the post-exilic time of tribulation and distress (Friday). For example, the Sunday prayer retells Genesis 1—2: 'Adam, our father, you fashioned in the image of your Glory . . . the breath of life you blew into his nostrils and intelligence and knowledge . . . in the Garden of Eden' (4Q504 8 4–6). This narrative section of each prayer is followed by a petition that often draws on themes articulated or implied in the narrative ('have pity on us . . . forgive our iniquity and our sin . . . strengthen our heart to do'). The conclusion is a blessing in which God is praised in relationship to the theme of the prayer (e.g. '[Blessed be] the Lord who taught us' (4Q504 4 14)). There is a communal response, 'amen, amen', further evidence of liturgical usage.

4Q504 is one of the earliest manuscripts preserved at Qumran. It was copied in the first part of the second century BC (perhaps 175–150 BC) and the prayers were composed even earlier (there is no reason to think this copy is the autograph). The very early date (even before the Teacher of Righteousness and the formation of the community) and the fact that there is nothing distinctively sectarian in the vocabulary and content (not the dualism, light/darkness language or any of special vocabulary of the *Thanksgiving Psalms*) leads to the conclusion that already in the second century BC at least some pious groups recited set daily prayers, a practice that was continued by the Essenes but did not originate with them. If this understanding is correct, we have here much earlier evidence for daily prayer than we had before, or than most scholars had postulated. It means that the practice of set communal prayer began while the temple was still standing, and not just as a response to the destruction of the temple in AD 70.

The prayer for the Sabbath in the *Words of the Luminaries* is quite different from that for the other days of the week. It is formulated in parallel poetic lines rather than as prose; it focuses on themes of creation and covenant; and it is totally doxological, with no petition/supplication. In Jewish prayer today, there is a distinction between the daily prayer which has as its core the *Eighteen Benedictions*, many of them petitionary in content, and the Sabbath *Amida* with seven benedictions, all of praise. The rabbis, too, had admonished against 'crying out' in petition on the Sabbath. Now we can see that this understanding of Sabbath as a day solely for praise goes much further back, at least to the second century BC.

Another type of prayer for the Sabbath is found in the *Songs of the Sabbath Sacrifice*. Nine copies of this work were found at Qumran (4Q400–407, 11Q17) and another copy in the ruins of Masada – obviously it was an important work. There are 13 compositions for consecutive Sabbaths, each beginning with a heading, 'By the *Maskil* [Instructor]. Song of the sacrifice of the x-Sabbath on the x-day of the x-month'. This is a very different type of prayer, as illustrated by the following selection from the song for the sixth Sabbath:

For the Instructor. Song of the sacrifice of the sixth Sabbath on the ninth of the second month. [Praise the] God of gods. O you inhabitants of the height of heights . . .

Psalm of blessing by the tongue of the first of the chief princes to the eternal God with its seven wondrous blessings; he will bless the King . . . seven times with seven words of wondrous blessing.

Psalm of magnification by the tongue of the second to the king of truth with its seven wondrous songs of magnification; and he will magnify the God of all the heavenly beings . . . seven times with seven words of wondrous magnification.

Psalm of exaltation by the tongue of the third of the chief princes . . . exalting the God of lofty angels seven times with seven words of wondrous exaltation . . .

And after going through all the seven chief princes, the same series is repeated with the seven deputy princes! This is a special type of language, like a chant, highly repetitive and formulistic, with long streams of nouns and adjectives that are almost impossible to translate. The final section, songs 9–13, work their way through an elaborate description of the heavenly temple, including the chariot-throne (*merkavah*) and the dress and worship of the angelic priesthood.

The origin and purpose of these songs is much debated. The discovery of one copy at Masada in addition to those found at Qumran needs to be taken into consideration. At first when scholars looked at these songs, they seemed so unusual in form and content that it was assumed they must have been composed by the Essenes and a copy taken to Masada by some survivors from Qumran. But the opposite could well be the case: these songs could have been brought to Masada by non-Essene Jews who were also using them, especially priests or others with a special interest in the esoteric and the heavenly realms. There are striking similarities with a body of literature that previously we only knew from some centuries later, the so-called *hekalot* hymns from mystical circles, which are concerned with esoteric practices that would allow the initiate to penetrate into the divine realm and encounter the heavenly chariot. Carol Newsom, the principal editor of the *Sabbath Songs*, has suggested that the repetitious, almost hypnotic language was intended precisely to produce a kind of 'communal mysticism', to give the reciters an experiential sense of participating in the heavenly cult even if they were priests who were presently shut out from the earthly temple.[9]

## The Annual Covenant Ceremony

The ritual that we have the most information about – albeit still very limited information – is the Annual Covenant Ceremony. This was a liturgy for the annual ceremony of the renewal of the covenant that was held during the feast of Weeks (Pentecost), on the fifteenth day of the third month, in the spring (the date is mentioned in various texts, including a fragment of the *Damascus Document* from cave 4). At this time new initiates took their solemn oath, all members renewed their commitment and received their ranking, and any member who rejected the communal discipline was expelled. This liturgy, including some of the actual words to be said, is given in some detail in the *Rule of the Community* (1QS 1 18–2 18). The ceremony illustrates two things: first, that new rituals could be, indeed had to be, developed to express the distinctive theology of this group, namely that as individuals they had been chosen by God to enter voluntarily into a 'new covenant' (CD 6 19), like the covenant made on Sinai based on the Law of Moses but now properly interpreted by the Teacher of Righteousness; and second, that these new liturgies were always in some way an adaptation of earlier biblical models. In the ritual for entrance into the covenant, the priests and Levites first 'bless the God of salvation and all his faithfulness', and all those who enter the covenant give their assent with a double 'amen, amen'. The priests then recite 'all the favours of God manifested in his mighty deeds and declare all his merciful grace to Israel', and the Levites recite 'all the iniquities of the children of Israel, all their guilty rebellions and sins during the dominion of Belial'. Those entering the covenant confess their sins: 'We have strayed, we have [disobeyed], we and our fathers before us have sinned and done wickedly . . .' (1QS 1 21–5), and then declare God's justice, '[And God has] judged us and our fathers'. This pattern of confession of sin combined with affirmation of divine justice is attested in penitential prayers from the post-exilic period (Dan. 9, Neh. 9, Ezra 9, 1 Kings 8). The service continues following the pattern of Deuteronomy 27–28, which described the solemn recitation of blessings and curses on Mt Gerizim and Mt Ebal. Here the priests recite blessings for those of God's lot, and the priests and Levites recite curses against those of the lot of Belial and those who attempt to enter the covenant falsely and insincerely. In the blessings, the priestly blessing of Numbers 6 is expanded and adapted to the community's dualistic theology and emphasis on knowledge:

> May he bless you *with all good* and preserve you *from all evil*;
> May he lighten your heart *with life-giving wisdom*, and grant you *eternal knowledge*;
> May he raise his merciful face towards you *for everlasting bliss*. (1QS 2 2–4)

It is in this covenant renewal that we can see most clearly how traditional biblical materials and specific sectarian beliefs could be brought together to create a new liturgical ceremony.

## Psalms: Poetry as Prayer

Finally, let us take a look at the various collections of religious poetry. Of special importance are the two copies of the *Thanksgiving Psalms* from cave 1 that we have already discussed, plus the six other copies of the *Thanksgiving Psalms* from cave 4. Many years ago (already in 1956), John Strugnell noted that these cave 4 manuscripts are very important because they 'fill in some lacunae and indicate that the order of the psalms was different'.[10] Strugnell and Hartmut Stegemann worked for many years on editing these cave 4 copies and I then took up the task in 1990, with final publication in 1999 (*DJD* XXIX). In some of these copies, it is clear that the individual psalms are arranged in a quite different order than in 1QHª, and there is at least one psalm in 4QHª that is not found in 1QHª. By attempting to reconstruct the shape of each cave 4 manuscript and determine its length, I think I can demonstrate that some were copies of smaller collections. For instance, 4QHᶜ is a very small scroll, less than eight centimetres in height with very narrow columns; to write out all the psalms of 1QHª in this format would require over 450 metres, creating a scroll that would be materially impossible to roll up and to use. There is good evidence to suggest that 4QHᶜ contained only the Hymns of the Teacher section of the whole *Thanksgiving Scroll*. What this demonstrates is that we are dealing with a much more complex collection than we had first realized, and it will require much further study to figure out all the various sub-collections and try to explain how and why they were brought together.

In addition to the *Thanksgiving Psalms*, and the collection(s) of the psalms of kings and prophets that we discussed earlier (4Q380, 381), there is still another collection named after the beginning of (at least) one of the psalms, *Barki Naphshi*, 'Bless the Lord, my soul' (as in Pss 103 and 104). Found in five copies (4Q434–38), these are more generalized psalms of thanksgiving and praise for divine deliverance and grace. It is very hard to know whether these were specific compositions of the Essene community or whether they had a broader base and usage within 'mainstream' Judaism.

# What Have We Learned About Prayer and Worship?

Especially interesting are various collections of psalms for getting rid of evil spirits (11QapocrPs, 4Q444, 8Q5, 4Q510–11). A few of these are incantations that bid the evil spirits to flee by addressing them directly: 'Who are you? . . . your face is a face of [nothin]g and your horns are horns of [dream]. [You ar]e darkness and not light; [injustic]e and not righteousness' (11QapPs 5 6–8). The 'Songs of the Sage' (4Q510–11), in contrast, are not typical words of admonition and dismissal but rather hymnic words of praise directed to God with the stated purpose to 'frighten and to terrify all the spirits of the angels of destruction and the spirits of bastards, demons, Lilith, howling creatures . . .' (4Q510 1 4–5). That is, the singing of hymns can function 'to spread the fear of God, [to terrify] with his power all the spirits of the bastards, to subjugate them not for all [eternal] times but for the times of their domination' (4Q511 35 6–8). As in the New Testament, this reflects a worldview that assumes the existence and power (real but subordinate) of demons and evil spirits.

Some psalms are not part of a psalmic collection but inserted in the midst of a narrative. This combination is, of course, known from the Bible, for example the song of Hannah (1 Sam. 2), the psalm of Jonah (Jonah 2), the psalm in praise of Jerusalem at the end of the book of Tobit (Tob. 13). In *Narrative and Poetry Composition* (4Q371–2),[11] we have a historical-like narrative recounting of the dispersion of the northern tribes, and then the transition to an extended poetic lament:

And for all this, Joseph [was put] into the hands of strangers to consume his strength and break his bones until the time of his end . . . he cried to the mighty God that he should save him from their hands. He said, 'My father and my God do

73

not abandon me to the hands of the nations. (4Q372 1 15–16)

The address to God, 'My father and my God', is significant. This is one of the few pre-Christian texts where God is directly addressed in prayer as 'father'; interestingly a second example is found in a similar text of narrative and petition (4Q 360 9 i 6, where the prayer ends 'my father and my Lord'). These texts illustrate a Jewish precedence for the address to God as father that we find in the Lord's Prayer (Matt. 6.9) and in the prayer of Jesus in Gethsemane (Matt. 26.39) and for Paul's encouragement to the early Christians to call on God as *abba* (Rom. 8.15; Gal. 4.6).

Finally, in addition to all this 'new' prayer material recovered from the scrolls, we should not forget the more than 30 manuscripts of the biblical Psalms. As we noted in the last chapter, there are far more copies of the psalms than there are of any other biblical book. Why so many copies? On the one hand, the psalms were considered to be words of prophecy that were being fulfilled now in the events associated with the foundation of their community. The psalms were studied and interpreted along with the prophetic books, and commentaries (*pesharim*) were written on the Psalter (4Q171, 173) just as they were written on the words of Isaiah, Hosea or Habakkuk. The more interesting question is whether the psalms were also used liturgically: that is, whether they were not only studied but also sung, perhaps to musical accompaniment. When we reconstruct the worship services, can we imagine both the recitation of the short blessing or petitionary prayers that we examined earlier and the singing of the biblical psalms, perhaps along with poems composed by the community (including the *Thanksgiving Psalms*)? Certainly that sort of combination is attested in Jewish prayer today and in much of Christian worship. Often it has been taken for granted that at the time of Jesus the psalms were a regular, set part of the synagogue service, and that this usage was passed on to the early church which adopted the three elements of the reading of scripture, homiletic exposition and psalmody in the Liturgy of the Word, with psalmody forming the core of the Divine Office. Indeed musicologists like Eric Werner have suggested that even the melodies of church chant came from synagogue cantillation.[12] Yet other scholars who study the historical development of Jewish liturgy are much more cautious. They judge that the regular fixed use of psalms came into the synagogue service relatively late, not until the fifth or sixth century.[13] This does not necessarily lead us to conclude that the Essenes did not sing the psalms in their services, but if they did this would be yet another example of how their worship was closer to that of the temple (where psalms had a place) rather than the synagogue. There is little clear manuscript evidence for the liturgical use of the psalms, although there might be some hints. For example, on one Psalms manuscript from cave 2 the first two lines of Psalm 103 were written in red ink, which could indicate a liturgical rubric (there might be another example of such a use of red ink in 4QNum[b]). But again, this is an area that needs further study.

## Conclusion

The caves at Qumran have provided us with a large body of prayer texts that we had no knowledge of previously. We have learned that there was an ongoing tradition of psalmic composition, as well as the development of shorter, prose prayers that followed certain formulaic patterns. It has taken scholars much of this first 50 years since the discovery to do the difficult and tedious work of editing and publishing the fragmentary bits and pieces. But as this technical stage draws to a close, the focus for future study can turn now to broader issues – and here I highlight only three.

First, though it seems obvious that prayers and psalms are an important resource for the study of the 'religion of the Dead Sea Scrolls', surprisingly little attention has been devoted to a theological reading of these texts.[14] There are, of course, dangers in attempting to abstract 'beliefs' from prayers. The language of devotion is fundamentally different from the language of dogmatics, and a religious poem is not a systematic treatise.[15] We need to think more about how the distinctive Essene theology and worldview found expression in, and influenced the shape of, their prayers.

Second, these prayers are of great value for studying the historical development of Jewish liturgy. The relationships are complex, especially since there was no direct link between this community and the groups that survived the destruction of the temple in AD 70 and shaped the standard prayer book over the next millennium, when they too (like the Essenes had done prior to AD 70) developed a form of worship (*avodah*) apart from the temple. Yet we can now see that the structure of prayers as blessings, the avoidance of petition on the Sabbath, even certain specific expressions used in the prayer book, clearly go back to the second century BC. Further progress will require that scholars who are experts in the history of Jewish liturgy become familiar with these new scrolls materials and that scrolls scholars think ahead as well as back in looking for links and similarities.

Third, there is much still to be studied in relation to

Christian liturgy. We have touched on only a few areas where there are obvious points of contact: the development of formal patterns of blessing and thanksgiving, the cosmic dimensions of prayer, the place of the meal, the use of psalmody, and prayer and praise against demons. In addition, the discipline of ritual studies can bring awareness of how ritual functions, of the use of language to establish boundaries, to include and to exclude, to establish hierarchy and power.[16] Again, this will call for the breaking down of traditional barriers between standard scholarly fields and more interdisciplinary work in order to exploit fully the rich potential of the texts that are now available to us.

## Notes

1. Eileen M. Schuller, *Non-Canonical Psalms from Qumran: A Pseudepigraphic Collection.* Later these manuscripts became part of *DJD* XI, pp. 75–172.

2. The terminology is not well defined. Sometimes a given text is called a 'psalm' by one author, a 'hymn' by another, and a third might put it under the more general category of 'prayer'. Often there is little strictly form-critical analysis, and texts are given designations based much more on a sense of 'well, this is what we would call it in my church/synagogue'. I will use the term 'psalm' broadly for poetic texts that are modelled in some general way on the individual compositions of the biblical Psalter. 'Prayer' will be used for prose compositions, often (but not always) of petition. I will reserve 'hymn' for compositions of praise that speak of God in the third person (for example, 'Praise the Lord, all you nations').

3. There is a special problem with regard to the large manuscript from cave 1 (1QH[a]) in terms of the column and line numbers. Both Hartmut Stegemann and Émile Puech, working independently, were able to reconstruct the original order of the columns (28 columns in total), and the placement of many of the smaller fragments can be established with much certainty (based on corresponding shapes of damages in

adjacent columns). This restored order is followed in recent translations (like that of Vermes, *The Complete Dead Sea Scrolls in English*); older translations and earlier editions of Vermes follow the column order established by Eleazer Sukenik, in *The Treasure of the Hidden Scrolls*. There is still a certain amount of confusion and variation in the line numbers, and citations will often differ by a few lines.

4. These fragments were taken to the Scrollery and were published by J. T. Milik in the first volume of *DJD* in 1955. Milik recognized the similiarity of these small bits to the sections he knew at that time of Sukenik's scroll and thought that they might actually belong to it. When all of Sukenik's scroll became accessible, it was apparent that there were actual overlaps, that is, this is a second copy of the same text.

5. Esther Chazon, 'Prayers from Qumran and their Historical Implications', *DSD* 1 (1994), 265–84.

6. Bilhah Nitzan, *Qumran Prayer and Religious Poetry*. The other major book-length study is by Daniel Falk, *Daily Sabbath and Festival Prayers in the Dead Sea Scrolls*. For a short commentary on selected texts see James R. Davila, *Liturgical Works*.

7. Annette Steudel, 'The Houses of Prostration CD xi 21–xii 1 – Duplicates of the Temple', *RQ* 16 (1993–94), 49–68.

8. I have discussed the blessings and their importance in an article, 'Some Observations on Blessings of God in Texts from Qumran' in *Of Scribes and Scrolls: Studies on the Hebrew Bible, Intertestamental Judaism and Christian Origins Presented to John Strugnell*, pp. 133–44.

9. Newsom, *Songs of the Sabbath Sacrifice*, especially pp. 71–2.

10. John Strugnell, 'Le travail d'édition des manuscrits de Qumrân', *RB* 63 (1956), 64.

11. This work was formerly called 'A Joseph Apocryphon' and that is the title used by Vermes in *The Complete Dead Sea Scrolls in English*, pp. 530–1.

12. Eric Werner's extensive study of musical influence was compiled in *The Sacred Bridge: Liturgical Parallels in the Synagogue and the Early Church*.

13. This is the conclusion of Lawrence A. Hoffman, *The Canonization of the Synagogue Service*.

14. For a preliminary attempt, see my essay 'Petitionary Prayer and the Religion of Qumran' in John J. Collins and Robert Kugler (eds), *Religion in the Dead Sea Scrolls*, pp. 29–45.

15. As someone has said about Christian hymnody, 'Christians will sing any heresy as long as it rhymes.'

16. For example, Robert Kugler has recently explored how the theoretical framework and categories of Catherine Bell might be used in describing the ritual life at Qumran in 'Making All Experience Religious: The Hegemony of Ritual at Qumran', *JSJ* 33 (2002), 131–52.

# 4

# What Have We Learned About Women?

That there could be – much less should be – a chapter on women in a volume about the Dead Sea Scrolls has not always been obvious. Whatever treasures the scrolls might contain, 50 years ago people would not have expected to learn much, if anything, about women from these texts. Indeed, among the things that made the scrolls distinctive was the fact that they seemed to reflect the world of male, celibate ascetics who had fled to the wilderness, men who eschewed 'normal society' in expectation of the imminent end of days and the final intervention of God. The scrolls might be expected to give us all sorts of new information about dualism, angelology, eschatology and messianism, but hardly about mundane, this-worldly concerns related to women, marriage and family life.

This interpretative framework was already set in place at the time of the first press release from the American School of Oriental Research in 1948 which identified one of the scrolls from cave 1 as 'a manual of discipline of some comparatively little-known sect or monastic order, possibly the Essenes' (see pp. 2 and 5 above). Prior to the discovery of the scrolls, the Essenes had been a mysterious, esoteric group, known only from the descriptions of the Jewish historian Josephus, the

Alexandrian philosopher Philo and the Roman historian Pliny.[1] Though their descriptions differ in details and in perspective (Philo had probably never met an Essene; Josephus claimed to have actually lived with them briefly as a young man), the one thing that all three classical writers could agree on was that this group of Jews did not include women. Pliny the Elder described the Essenes as living to the west of the Dead Sea, 'a people unique of its kind and admirable beyond all others in the whole world, without women and renouncing love entirely, without money, and having for company only the palm trees' (*National History* 5.17, 4). Philo stated categorically, 'No Essaean takes a wife.' (*Hypothetica* 14). Josephus explained that they 'disdain marriage for themselves . . . they are on their guard against the licentiousness of women and are convinced that none of them is faithful to one man' (*The Jewish War* 2.120–1). Yet, after going on in such vein for considerable length, Josephus unexpectedly ends up with a brief reference to the existence of 'another order of Essenes who, although in agreement with the others on the way of life, usages, and customs', do marry for the sake of 'the propagation of the human race', since 'if everyone adopted the same opinion the race would very quickly disappear' (*The Jewish War* 2.160).

When the first batch of scrolls from cave 1 was read, they seemed to reinforce the links, even the identity, of the authors of the scrolls with the Essenes. The *Rule of the Community* makes no mention of women, sexual relations, marriage or family; there is no vocabulary related to females or procreation except for traditional biblical idioms, 'the son of your handmaid; one born of a woman' (1QS 11 16, 21), and a metaphorical hope for 'fruitfulness of seed' (1QS 4 7). In the *War Scroll*, the detailed battle plan for the future war of the Sons of Light versus the Sons of Darkness, women are mentioned only once, by way of exclusion: 'no boy or woman shall enter their camps from the time they leave Jerusalem and march out to war until they return' (1QM 7 3). In the *Thanksgiving Psalms*, women appear metaphorically (for example, the pregnant woman giving birth to a male child/community, 1QH^a 11 7–12), but the psalmist and his companions who are giving thanks and receiving revelatory knowledge all seem to be male.

Yet even in the early days of scrolls research, there were at least a few hints that the total picture was more complex. Two additional sheets that had been broken off from the scroll containing the *Rule of the Community* were found in the excavation of cave 1 and published in 1955 in *DJD* I. The first contained another, shorter rulebook that begins, 'This is the rule for all the congregation of Israel in the last days' (1QSa 1 1) and goes on to detail a whole series of regulations. Here it is assumed that a man will marry, the question is at what age: 'he shall not [approach] a woman to know her by lying with her before he is fully twenty years old' (1QSa 1 10). In another place, the *Rule of the Congregation* speaks of an assembly of the whole congregation: 'They shall summon them all, the little children and the women also' for the reading of the Torah and the exposition of their statutes 'so that they may no longer stray in their [errors]' (1QSa 1 4). Whether these 'last days' are understood as the present time or as a distant eschatological future still to come, in this rule it is simply taken for granted that women will be present and active participants in the life of the congregation.

In the 1950s when archaeologists turned their attention to the ruins near to the caves at Khirbet Qumran, the physical remains they uncovered revealed large communal buildings, with a centralized kitchen and massive dining hall, not individual family units. When a portion of the cemetery of about 1,200 graves adjacent to the site was excavated, the results seemed to confirm that this was a celibate male community. Roland de Vaux, the archaeologist responsible for the excavations, concluded that 'all the skeletons in that part of the cemetery which is carefully planned [the so-called 'main cemetery'] are male'.[2] Admittedly there were a few graves excavated that yielded the remains of women and children, but de Vaux argued that these were located in fringe, outlying areas that were extensions or secondary areas of burial. De Vaux and subsequent scholars were never quite sure what to make of these women and children in light of their paradigm of a male, celibate community occupying the site. Were these mothers who came to visit? Housekeeping staff? A few particularly devout and pious women who chose to be buried out in this desert centre rather than in their family tombs?

In the 1950s and 60s, then, and well into the 1970s and 80s, women were largely absent from the world of the texts and of archaeology, and the few undeniable traces of their presence were pushed to the periphery, virtually ignored. But in the last 15 or 20 years, the situation has changed slowly but dramatically. More and more texts have been published that mention women specifically, or that treat of topics like childbirth, menstruation and regulations concerning sexual relations between men and women. Because of the random way in which individual manuscripts were published over so many years and by many different scholars, it has taken a while to realize just how much material the scrolls actually contain about women. Certainly it is only in recent years that the topic of 'women in the scrolls' has become a matter for study in its own right.

Perhaps I can mention my own experience to illustrate the turn-about in attitude. In the early 1990s, the Canadian Society of Biblical Studies was engaged in an ongoing seminar on Voluntary Associations (clubs, *collegia*, associations) in the ancient world.[3] In 1992, the specific topic was the role of women in such associations, and various scholars were asked to contribute half-hour papers on specific aspects such as 'Women in the Cult of Isis', 'Women in the *Ekklesia* at Corinth', 'Women in the Greek Philosophical Schools'. One of the organizers called me and asked if I would present a paper on 'Women in the Dead Sea Scrolls' – and laughed, saying I could do whatever I wanted to fill up the remaining 20 minutes! Ten years later, in 2002, for the annual meeting of the Society of Biblical Literature, I was approached again. This time it was to give a response to a three-hour plenary panel session, five papers on Women at Qumran, papers given by leading Qumran scholars (interestingly all men).[4] In the last ten years, this has come to be recognized as an important issue in scrolls scholarship per se – and not just the special hobby of a few women with feminist interests. But this area of research is still in an early stage of development; much work remains to be done both in terms of detailed study of specific texts and in fine-tuning the overall methodological sophistication we bring to this study.

## The Nature of the Evidence

Before we turn to an examination of some specific texts, a few general observations may be helpful. A quick scan through the scrolls indicates that there are no passages that explicitly discuss what the authors thought about women, about relationship between the sexes, or appropriate roles for women in the family, community and broader society. There are no programmatic statements about the nature of women such as found in Philo: 'Women are selfish, jealous, skilful in ensnaring the morals of a spouse and in seducing him by endless charms. Women set out to flatter . . . when they have deceived the lower senses, they next lead the sovereign mind astray' (*Hypothetica* 14–15); or as we read earlier in Josephus, 'they [the Essenes] are on their guard against the licentiousness of women and are convinced that none of them is faithful to one man' (*The Jewish War* 2.121).

There is only one woman named in the corpus of nonbiblical texts, Shelamzion, the Hasmonean queen Alexandra Salome (as she is called in Greek sources) who ruled from 76 to 67 BC. Her name appears in a very fragmentary calendrical list of memorial days (4Q320 2 4 and 4Q324 1 5), but the text is so broken that we do not even know whether the day that commemorated some event associated with her was an occasion for joy or for sorrow.

I know of only one place where a woman is addressed directly: a very fragmentary section of a long wisdom text (much like the book of Proverbs), *Instruction*, where an unnamed woman is given rather conventional wisdom-type instruction about her relationship to her husband and father-in-law: 'Honour [him, i.e. your father-in-law] like your father . . . do not remove in your heart . . . lest you neglect [your] holy covenant . . . from the house where you were born' (4Q415 2 ii 1–9). Furthermore, there may be a handful of texts, at best, where a woman is the speaker. One is in a very puzzling document, 4Q502, describing a ritual ceremony of celebration and joy in which women have a part: sisters, old women, virgins and young girls are named. In one fragment, a woman stands in the council of 'old men and old women' (or, if these are titles perhaps we should translate 'male Elders and female Elders') and seems to address the men: 'Your (masculine pronoun) years in peace' (4Q502 24 5).[5] The editor of these 344 tiny bits of papyrus thought this might be describing a wedding ceremony, but it could also be a New Year festival or some other special ceremony.[6]

Texts that are primary for our consideration (for both what they contain and what they do not contain) belong to the genre of 'Rule of Life' or 'Constitutional Rule' (e.g. *Damascus Document*, *Rule of the Community*, *Rule of the Congregation*) or collections of specific sectarian regulations for the correct interpretation of Torah (e.g. the *Temple Scroll*, *Some Observances of the Law* [4QMMT], *Tohorot* [Purities] and *Ordinances*). One of the most complex questions in scrolls study today is the relationship of all these texts to one another. To state the question rather bluntly: do all these documents pertain to or originate from the same group within Palestinian Judaism? The dominant 'working scenario' in much of scrolls scholarship over the past decades has been that the *Rule of the Community* (S) was the rule for a celibate male group (the *yahad*) living at the site of Qumran that did not marry, while the *Damascus Document* (D) prescribed regulations for 'the camps' scattered throughout the land where marriage and family life were the norm; yet there was obviously some relationship between the *yahad* and the 'camps' in various places if for no other reason than that multiple copies of the *Damascus Document* were found at Qumran. Where the *Rule of the Congregation* (1QSa) 'fits' is less clear: some scholars consider that it was the rule in the early stages when marriage and family life was the norm; others read it as regulations for a future restored Israel at the 'end of the days'. The issue becomes even more complex with the recent publication of multiple copies of the *Rule of the Community* from cave 4 which show that the *Rule of the Community* was itself a complex, composite document that went through various stages of development. At present, we can speak more confidently about women in a particular document, for example women in the *Damascus Document*, but it is far from clear how to combine – or even if we should combine – the evidence of each individual document plus small fragmentary bits and pieces to try to come up with some comprehensive picture.

Yet we do need some working hypothesis, particularly to decide how we will use the relevant passages from Josephus, Philo and Pliny. For our purposes here, let us assume that the scrolls are coming from a broad movement within Second Temple Judaism, of which the specific group at Qumran was only a segment. Perhaps the site of Qumran was a desert retreat for the elite, 'all those who walk . . . in perfect holiness' (CD 7 5), and/or a place of intensive training for new members. Josephus and Philo never mention Qumran or the desert, but rather describe the Essenes as living 'in every town and village'. They were probably married. That is why there is no explicit mention of celibacy, nor is there any attempt to counter the fundamental Genesis commandment to 'be fruitful and multiply' (Gen. 1.28). Perhaps a small sub-group did not marry, choosing to be celibate in order to maintain a higher, consistent level of purity and to be always ready as warriors for the final eschatological battle. If the various Rules are somehow to be read together in light of one another (and they were all found in the caves), perhaps it is not so significant that the *Rule of the Community* does not mention women explicitly. After all, this particular document does not mention Sabbath or Sabbath observance either, but no one concludes from this that these were not Sabbath-observant Jews.

A final methodological issue: if we allow that many of the documents assume a community that includes women, should we be limiting our survey to passages that mention women specifically? In discussing the topic of women, the first impulse is to do a search of the concordance for words like woman, virgin, widow, maidservant – but is that sufficient? All our texts are fundamentally androcentric in perspective and formulation; that is, as in the biblical law codes, regulations are regularly formulated in the masculine (unless they apply only to women, e.g. concerning childbirth). But such regulations, though expressed in masculine grammatical forms, can apply also to women and thus they form part of the corpus of texts about women. For example, if we assume that the *Damascus Document* is an exhortation to the whole community, the translation, 'and now, children, listen to me' (CD 2 14) is more accurate than 'and now, sons (*benim*), listen to me'.[7] Similarly there is a sense in which the *Thanksgiving Psalms*, especially the Hymns of the Community, could be included in our survey as psalms that reflect the piety of women as well as of men. Even though we will focus our attention in the rest of this chapter on passages that specifically mention women, it is important to state explicitly that these are certainly not the only passages that were relevant to those women who had 'freely devoted themselves to the observance of God's precepts' (1QS 1 7) within this framework.

## Marriage and Divorce

A large number of the specific regulations that involve women deal with issues of marriage, sexual relations, menstruation and childbirth. All of these are difficult texts, and we cannot discuss every issue or possible interpretation here, but this short overview can give some sense of the nature and complexity of the material at our disposal.

According to a key passage in the Admonition section of the *Damascus Document* (CD 4 12–5 11), the authors of the *Damascus Document* defined themselves in contrast to other Jews, the 'builders of the wall', who are ensnared in the 'three nets of Belial'. Although the way these three nets are subsequently explained is intricate and not always clear, what is striking is that it was issues of who to marry or not marry (not one's niece), of divorce and remarriage (forbidden) and of sexual relations (in relation to menstruation) – all issues involving women – that were the core of the community's self-definition vis-à-vis the rest of Judaism which is accused of following corrupt practices on these points.

One of the things that 'they/the bad guys' do is 'to take two wives in their (masculine) lifetime' (CD 4 20–1); by implication, this community does not do this. But does not do what? 'To take two wives' can be interpreted in different ways. In the simplest and most lenient interpretation, this is a prohibition of polygamy/taking two wives at the same time. This was permitted in biblical practice, and there are some incidents of polygamy attested from the Greco-Roman period, especially among the elite classes, but it does not seem as if the practice was widespread enough to make this a defining issue of identity. Most scholars have argued that what is at stake is divorce, or more precisely, remarriage after divorce. That is, this group of Jews, in contrast to the Pharisees and later rabbinic practice, forbade divorce or remarriage after divorce. It is not quite that simple, however, because there are other passages in the *Damascus Document* that seem to permit divorce; at least one text specifies that one of the duties of the Overseer of the whole camp is to give 'counsel to the one who divorces' (CD 13 17 and 4Q266 9 iii 5). The third, the strictest interpretation, would be that 'not to take two wives in their lifetime' forbids a man to remarry ever, even after the death of his spouse: literally men cannot have two wives ever, no matter what the circumstances.

Which of these three prohibitions is at stake here – polygamy, remarriage after divorce, or remarriage after the death of a wife – is still a matter of much debate among scholars. But even if the precise interpretation is uncertain, we can learn much from this passage. First of all, it is clear that issues of marriage and divorce were disputed in Second Temple Judaism. 'Those caught in the nets of Belial' do one thing; this group understands that the Torah of Moses is to be interpreted in quite a different way. They quote biblical texts as proof: 'male and female he created them' (Gen. 1.27 quoted in CD 4 21) and 'they went into the ark two by two' (Gen. 7.9 in CD 5 1). We can recall the text in the Gospel of Matthew where the Pharisees come to Jesus and ask, 'Is it lawful for a man to divorce his wife for any cause?' (Matt. 19.3; also Mark 10.2). Before the discovery of the scrolls, New Testament scholars often viewed this question as artificial, a purely literary device, something no one would have ever thought to ask in real life. After all, Deuteronomy 24.1 takes it for granted that divorce is allowed, at least under certain circumstances; different groups of Pharisees (the House of Hillel, the House of Shammai) debated not about divorce per se but about what might be sufficient cause. So why should anyone approach Jesus to ask, 'Is it lawful for a man to divorce his wife?' Now we can see that people did argue about this issue and how the relevant scriptural texts were to be interpreted, and this is one instance where the strict teaching of Jesus was closer to that of the Qumran group than to the Pharisees.

But there is another question that is usually not even voiced in scholarly discussion of this passage: how were women affected by this particular interpretation of the Torah? Note that the regulation itself (as most biblical law) was formulated from the perspective of the man – but it affected the lives of women also. Was strictness regarding divorce perceived as security for the woman – or as a condemnation to an abusive situation? If remarriage after divorce was disallowed, did this create a category of 'unattached women' who did not have a place within the family system? What was the social status of these women? Stegemann has suggested that this regulation was the reason why Josephus was able to present the Essenes as unmarried: if women frequently died young in childbirth and men could not remarry, a large number of the community would *de facto* have been men without wives.[8] In asking questions such as this, we are making the leap from text to recreating the social reality behind the text; we are assuming that real men and women were living these regulations, that this was not a utopian or theoretical formulation.

## Sexual Relations within Marriage

Throughout all the texts we are considering, it is assumed that men and women engage in sexual relations. There is no condemnation or prohibition of sexual activity, no suggestion that sex is evil or that female sexuality is particularly problematic. There is concern for purity, particularly with regard to the impurity caused by bodily discharges, but this applies to both men and women. Yet there are a number of cases where this community interprets biblical law differently from the Pharisaic/rabbinic interpretation, and the difference is almost always in the direction of greater strictness.

For example, according to the *Damascus Document*, the third net of Belial ensnares the rest of Israel and causes profanation of the temple 'because they do not observe the distinction [between clean and unclean] in accordance with the Law, but lie with a woman who sees her bloody discharge' (CD 5 6–7). This suggests that the authors followed a different (presumably stricter) practice with regard to intercourse and menstruation (and so they considered other Jews in violation of Levitical law). Another example is the prohibition of sexual intercourse in Jerusalem, 'No man shall lie with a woman in the city of the Sanctuary' (CD 12 1).[9] Yet another fragmentary text (4Q270 2 i 18) gives a long list of transgressors, among whom is 'one who approaches his wife on the day of [. . .'; the text breaks off right at this point. Joseph Baumgarten, when he edited these fragments, suggested restoring the text to 'on the [Sabbath] day'. That is, in this community sexual activity was forbidden on the Sabbath, whereas the rabbis praised and encouraged sexual pleasure on the Sabbath. A few lines later (4Q270 2 ii 16), the transgressor is 'one who lies with a pregnant woman causing blood to stir'. Again the meaning is not clear: is the concern here with blood because of purity, or a fear of doing harm to the foetus? The same regulation seems to be reflected in Josephus's statement about the marrying Essenes, 'and when they are pregnant they have no intercourse with them' (*The Jewish War* 2.161). A final example is from the Penal Code, a long list of offences and the penalties imposed. One of the most serious is the case of a man who 'draws near to his wife to act immorally (*liznot*) with her' (4Q270 7 i 13). Again, the precise nature of the offence is unclear but some type of sexual activity between a man and his wife is judged serious enough to merit the most extreme of all punishments, 'he shall depart and not return again'. These multiple restrictions on sexual activity may be related to Josephus's statement that even those who do marry 'do not marry for pleasure but because it is necessary to have children' (*The Jewish War* 2.161). Again, many of these regulations raise questions about what the focus on sexual activity for the purpose of childbearing meant for women, especially those who did not conceive.

There are further regulations in the *Damascus Document* that deal with purity/impurity in connection with menstruation and childbirth. Once more, the general thrust is greater stringency than in the rabbinic system. For example, a woman who has a flow of blood beyond the seven-day menstrual period (4Q266 6 ii 2–4) is considered as a *zabah* (in contrast to rabbinic and Samaritan halakhah which did not invoke the category of *zabah* unless the bleeding continued for a longer period of time). Another passage (4Q266 6 ii 5–13) speaks of the period of impurity after childbirth prescribed in Leviticus 12.1–8; the mention of a wet nurse may suggest that the mother could not nurse during the period of her impurity, but the passage is very fragmentary and other interpretations may be possible.

## Selection of a Husband

Another set of regulations that touch upon the lives of women in a most direct way (particularly given the strictures about divorce and remarriage) are the prescriptions concerning the selection of a marriage partner. The regulations are formulated from the perspective of the father who is charged with choosing a husband for his daughter. In another place, however, the Overseer of the whole community seems to have had some role in the selection (4Q266 9 iii 4–5, 'and thus for everyone who tak[es a wife], he is to act with counsel'). The traditional authority of the father was restricted when both men and women surrendered considerable personal autonomy to the authority of the community as a whole. The subject of marriage is introduced within the larger context of the laws concerned with fraud in carrying out a business transaction. In giving his daughter in marriage (4Q271 3 4–10), the father is to make a complete disclosure of her blemishes lest he bring upon himself the curse of one who makes the blind stumble (from Deut. 27.18 and Lev. 19.14). Nothing is said about the blemishes of the groom! To this is added the statement that her father should not give her to 'one unfit for her'. This exact expression is not attested elsewhere, and numerous suggestions have been offered about how to interpret it. Probably what is at issue here is that the husband-to-be must meet certain halakhic requirements (for example, he cannot be her uncle [CD 5 8] or a man less than the age of 20, 1QSa 1 9–11). Perhaps there is a concern for compatibility in age, learning or social status; we can recall the statement in the book of Tobit about Sarah's fitness as a bride for Tobias: 'she was set apart for you before the world was made' (Tob. 6.18). But this may be too sentimental an interpretation of 'fit for her'.

The passage continues: a man cannot marry a woman who has been sexually active before marriage, either as a young girl 'in her father's house' or as a widow after she was widowed. If there is a suspicion that the girl is not a virgin, 'let no man take her, except upon examination by trustworthy women of repute selected by command of the supervisor'. This is a specific interpretation of the laws of Deuteronomy 22. In the biblical text, the context is the husband who makes the accusation on his wedding night that his bride was not a virgin; if the charge is proved, according to Deuteronomy the woman is to be put to death. The interpretation of the law here disallows that possibility (the fact of virginity is settled before the wedding), and in that way protects the woman from the death penalty. Notice that it is assumed that there will be women who have the expertise to establish the fact of physical virginity and who are accepted by the community as 'reliable' (the same terminology is used here as for the male witnesses in CD 9 23 whose testimony is accepted).

## Position and Status

That women were present in the community is obvious from the passages that we have read. But could women choose independently to join this group, go through the same initiation rites and take the same 'oaths of the covenant' as did men – or were they part of the group only if they were born into it or through marriage to a man who was a member? Were they really 'members'/'full members'? Could they exercise any leadership roles? Were they equal to men? These are, of course, modern questions (equality is not a term that we find in the scrolls!), and very difficult to answer. But there are some hints that women had a certain status, and even positions of leadership.

The *Rule of the Congregation* (1QSa 1 10–11) has a short statement about the issue of giving witness, and not only the text itself but also how it has been treated by scholars is a fascinating study. The context is a list of appropriate ages for certain activities in the education of children: specifically the age for instruction in the 'book of *Hagu*' (some special book of rulings or meditation) and in the precepts of the covenant; the age for enrolment; and the age of marriage for the man: 'he shall not [approach] a woman to know her by lying with her before he is fully twenty years old when he shall know [good] and evil' (1QSa 1 10). (Nothing is said about the age of marriage for women, but it was probably younger.)[10] This is followed immediately by a statement about his wife: 'She shall be received to give witness concerning him about the regulations of the law and to take a place in the proclamation of the regulations.' The handwriting on the scroll is perfectly clear and legible at this point – there is no uncertainty that the first word is the feminine verbal form, 'she shall be received'.[11] Yet some of the first scholars who wrote on this text argued that it should read, 'he shall be received to give witness'. They said that it was impossible for women to give witness; this would be contrary to the rabbis and Jewish tradition, and so the text must be emended. Today most of these same scholars admit that such an emendation is methodologically unsound – we have to let the text say what it says.[12] This is not a blanket statement about the acceptance of testimony from a woman. It speaks specifically about testimony that she alone can give concerning marital relationships (testimony that the rabbis also did allow in specific circumstances). Thus, according to this regulation, a women's testimony can be accepted, and it is assumed that women are instructed and knowledgeable about the details of law in matters of sexual relations and purity.

Furthermore, in addition to those women whose skill and trustworthiness are recognized in determining the virginity of an unmarried girl (see p. 95 above), there is another group of women who seem to have been accorded some special recognition within the community. They are called 'the Mothers', and this clearly seems to be a title (hence my capitalization) like 'the Fathers'. The two terms occur only once, in a section of the penal code: '[If he has murmured] against the Fathers, he shall leave and shall not return [again]. But if he has murmured against the Mothers, he shall do penance for ten days. For the Mothers have no *rwqmh* (?) within the [Congregation]' (4Q270 7 i 13–14). An offence against the Fathers is paralleled with an offence against the Mothers. There is an obvious major discrepancy between the severities of the punishments: expulsion for those who murmur against the Fathers, ten-day punishment (probably food reduction) for those who murmur against the Mothers. Unfortunately, the final phrase of the passage has not yet been explained in any convincing manner. We simply do not know what *rwqmh* means; in some contexts it refers to variegated coloured cloth; in this context, it perhaps means something like 'authority' or 'status'.

## Celibacy

Given that the texts that refer to women most often do so in specific contexts of marriage, sexual relations and child-bearing, we can ask whether there is any text that envisions the possibility that some women may choose to remain unmarried. Indeed the same question can be asked about whether celibacy was a possible choice for men. Note the turn-around: in the early days of Qumran scholarship the question was posed as, 'Was anyone married in this community?' Now it is, 'Were any members unmarried?'

There is no passage that explicitly discusses celibacy, nor how the Torah commandment 'be fruitful and multiply' (Gen. 1.28) should be interpreted and whether or not it applied to women as well as men. There is one complex and seemingly disjointed passage in the *Damascus Document* (CD 6 11–7 9) that might be read as pointing to a bifurcation in the members. According to these lines, there is one group who 'will walk according to these precepts in perfect holiness, according to all the teaching of God', and these will be rewarded for their asceticism since 'the covenant of God shall be an assurance that they shall live for thousands of generations'. Another group is introduced with a disjunctive 'but if': 'But if they live in the camps according to the rule of the land, marrying and begetting children . . .' The whole passage is written from an androcentric perspective, but this does not disallow that there was a similar bifurcation of women: those 'who walk according to these matters in perfect holiness' in celibacy and the women who marry. Although there was often need to be explicit about the regulations for those who marry, little would need to be said explicitly about those women (perhaps a small number) not involved with marriage and childbirth, and so they were rendered virtually invisible.

# What Have We Learned About Women?

## The Evidence of Archaeology

We have already mentioned how scholars even in the 1950s had turned from texts to the ruins at the site of Khirbet Qumran and to the adjacent cemeteries in an attempt to recover more information about the occupants of the site, specifically the women. It should be noted that we are now talking about this particular site of Qumran, not other communities who lived in 'camps' and in 'towns and villages' which have not left any material traces.

When the ruins were first excavated, the size of the large assembly/dining hall (about 100 square metres), the 700 bowls in the pantry and the absence of multiple small dwellings suggested that the occupants of the site lived a communal lifestyle rather than in nuclear-family units. More recently the question has been raised whether other finds need to be considered, particularly those small objects distinctively associated with women: beads, ear rings, mirrors, jewellery, spindle whorls.[13] For instance, there is at least one, perhaps three, spindle whorls listed in the object catalogues from Qumran and Ein Feshka; their significance is dependent on the larger ongoing discussion among archaeologists and anthropologists about whether spinning was a specifically female occupation in antiquity. At present, few answers can be given to such questions of 'engendered archaeology' because most of the small material objects have not yet been published.

Of special importance in this discussion is the large cemetery of approximately 1,200 graves that lies some 30 to 40 metres east of the settlement, as well as two smaller cemeteries to the north and south. The normal practice in Second Temple Judaism, at least among the wealthy, was burial in the family tomb, with secondary collection and preservation of the bones of an individual in an ossuary (a box made of limestone, some-times with the name engraved). At Qumran, in contrast, the dead were buried in graves dug into the marl to a depth of approximately two metres, usually for a single inhumation. At the bottom of each grave, a niche was dug along the length of the shaft and the body was placed in this loculus, which was sealed with stone slabs or mud bricks. The shaft was then filled with earth and heaps of small stones put at one end and a larger stone at the other. Most of the graves had a north–south orientation; the occupant was presumably buried ready to rise facing north, the site of paradise in certain passages in *Enoch*.

Roland de Vaux excavated some 43 graves (one of his assistants is reported to have said that he quit then because the graves were so similar and boring). From these graves, five or six skeletons were identified as female by de Vaux, but it is often not at all clear how or by whom the identification male/female was made. In terms of the arrangement of the cemetery, as we noted above (p. 83), de Vaux concluded that in the central part of the cemetery where the graves were most regularized, only male skeletons were found. One female skeleton (T7) was recovered in this area but de Vaux claimed that it was in a position apart from the general alignment and is of a different type from the rest. Six other graves of women (and four of children) were found in what de Vaux called 'the extensions' to the main cemetery or in the two secondary ones.

In recent years, with the increasing interest in women, many archaeologists have wanted to study once again the skeletons excavated by de Vaux. The question began to be asked: how certain was it that all these skeletons – and only these – were female? Given that there was no final archaeological report, it was often difficult to find out if the identification had been made on the basis of the skull or pelvis or the whole skeleton, or because of the presence of beads or jewellery in a grave. But until very recently, nothing could be done to explore questions like these, since the skeletons had been 'lost'. Apart from one that was rumoured to be in the basement of the Rockefeller Museum, it was simply not known what had happened to the bones from de Vaux's excavations. Now in the last few years the skeletons have been 'found' – 22 are in Munich, 8 in a museum in Paris, and 9 in Jerusalem. In the last few years, these remains have been subject to examination using newer anthropological methods and criteria for determining gender.

There is still ongoing controversy about the results. Most archaeologists now think that the graves of women and children in the southern extension area (many of which were distinctive in containing beads and jewellery) are really modern Bedouin graves, and thus totally irrelevant to our concerns. In the main cemetery, there are perhaps three graves with females.[14] Whatever the exact number, the proportion is certainly much smaller than would be expected in a normal cemetery, and suggests that there was something unusual about the group who were burying their dead here.

But the proportion of graves that have been excavated, 43 out of approximately 1,200, less than 4 per cent of the total, is statistically so small as to make any conclusion almost meaningless.[15] Until all the graves, or at least a truly representative portion, are excavated and the contents scientifically examined, the cemetery cannot really be used in any meaningful way as an independent source of evidence about either the presence or the absence of women at the site of Qumran.

## For the Future

It is clear that much more work remains to be done on this topic. For the most part, the study of women in the scrolls has not been an integral part of the burgeoning and increasingly methodologically sophisticated feminist scholarship on women in classical antiquity, the Hebrew Bible, the New Testament, Second Temple Judaism and the Mishnah. The reasons for this are understandable. Few scrolls scholars have been interested in or experts in critical feminist scholarship, and few feminist scholars have had more than a superficial knowledge of the scrolls. Indeed, with all the problems until recent years of accessing and publishing texts, and because of the perception that scrolls research is an esoteric, highly specialized field best left to the experts, even books that claimed to deal precisely with 'Jewish Woman in Greco-Roman Palestine' (to quote the title and sub-title respectively of two recent works[16]) have treated the scrolls only in a most perfunctory manner.

Today, there is the opportunity for a more interdisciplinary study that will incorporate insights and methods learned from the feminist study of other texts of antiquity. In particular, a feminist-critical methodology can bring to our reading of the scrolls a more explicit awareness that the relationship between androcentric text and historical reality cannot be constructed as a mirror-image. While we have now collected a number of passages that speak about women, we are a long way from hearing the voice of the women who lived their lives according to the regulations and worldview of these texts.

Yet considering how little we know about women in antiquity overall, we can be grateful that the discovery of the scrolls has added a new and unexpected source of information. In this area, as in so many others, the scrolls have proven to be 'an absolutely incredible find'.

## Notes

1. The key texts in Greek and Latin are conveniently collected by Geza Vermes and Martin D. Goodman (eds), *The Essenes According to the Classical Sources*.

2. Roland de Vaux, *Archaeology and the Dead Sea Scrolls*, p. 47.

3. The results of the seminar have now been published as a volume edited by John S. Kloppenborg and Stephen G. Wilson, *Voluntary Associations in the Graeco-Roman World*.

4. Most of these papers have been collected and published in *DSD* 11/2 (2004), 167–261.

5. There may actually be mention of 'the woman, thanksgivings' at the top of the fragment, but the phrase is added interlineally and the division between words is not at all clear. The letters could also be divided to read 'the man, the thanksgivings'.

6. For example, Joseph Baumgarten proposed that this was a special ceremony in which older men and women, who had once been married, take on celibacy for the sake of greater purity or as a preparation for the final days ('4Q502, Marriage or Golden Age Ritual', *JJS* 34 [1983], 125–35).

7. This was recognized already by Chaim Rabin – who was hardly influenced by feminist concerns – in his translation in 1958, 'and now, children, hearken unto me', *The Zadokite Documents*, p. 8.

8. Hartmut Stegemann, *The Library of Qumran*, pp. 193–7.

9. Some scholars interpret the 'the city of the Sanctuary' as applying only to the Temple Mount (not the whole city of Jerusalem), but then, it is hard to see why this regulation would be necessary.

10. There is one passage in Josephus's description of the Essenes that might be interpreted to mean that a girl could be married after she has had three menstrual periods (*The Jewish War* 2.161), but the Greek is very uncertain here, and other interpretations are possible.

11. Possibly we could translate this in the active, 'she shall accept to give witness', rather than the passive, 'she shall be accepted to give witness'.

12. Even in the most recent edition of Geza Vermes, *The Complete*

*Dead Sea Scrolls in English*, the masculine translation still is retained: 'And thereafter, he shall be accepted when he calls to witness . . .'

13. See especially the discussion of Joan Taylor, 'The Cemeteries of Khirbet Qumran and Women's Presence at the Site', *DSD* 6 (1999), 317–21.

14. For a recent and accessible discussion, see the chapter on 'Women and the Cemetery at Qumran' by Jodi Magness in *The Archaeology of Qumran and the Dead Sea Scrolls*, pp. 163–87. Magness is drawing upon the work of the American anthropologist Susan Sheridan, who has done the most complete study of all the skeletons, especially those in Paris and Jerusalem.

15. Not included in this discussion are the ten graves, containing nine skeletons, excavated by Solomon H. Steckoll around 1966. His material has not been fully published nor is it available for study today, and the claims that he made are often unreliable.

16. For example, Léonie R. Archer, *Her Price is Beyond Rubies: The Jewish Woman in Greco-Roman Palestine*, or Tal Ilan, *Jewish Women and Greco-Roman Palestine: An Inquiry into Image and Status*.

# 5

# Looking to the Future

One stage of work on the Dead Sea Scrolls has now run its course and come to an end. The scrolls are all now (or will be in the very near future) available for study in both standard critical editions and English translation. There will, of course, continue to be refinements, re-edition of specific texts, identifications of some small pieces heretofore not associated with any previously known composition, occasionally perhaps a new join of two small fragments (or at least a join proposed) that the editors had not seen or judged to be certain. But the technical, time-consuming, painstaking work of preparing editions no longer will be at the centre of scrolls scholarship.

Perhaps there is something in the experience of 'turning 50' that calls forth the impulse to compile and consolidate what has been achieved. Such consolidation has found concrete expression in the rash of handbooks, textbooks and general surveys that have been written in the past ten years,[1] and above all, in the two-volume *Encyclopedia of the Dead Sea Scrolls* that appeared in 2000.[2] Since that time there has been a flurry of new projects, a whole spectrum of multi-volume series in the proposal stage or already in progress. Some are geared to a general, popular audience, but most are targeted more specifically at the undergraduate university audience and at those people who are now ready to go beyond the basic facts and explore specific topics or genres in greater depth.[3] Other projects are directed to specialists and scholars, such as the production (in both print and electronic form) of a complete Hebrew/Aramaic Concordance for the scrolls.[4] Eventually there will be full-length critical scholarly commentaries on the major Qumran documents in the international *Hermeneia* Commentary Series, the first time that the scrolls have been included in such a major biblical commentary series.[5] And, of course, we await the publication of the further volumes by scholars at the École Biblique et Archéologique Française de Jérusalem that will give us a complete archaeological report of the excavations of the 1950s and all the finds (pottery, glass, metals, coins), in accordance with standards that are normative in the field today.

Moving ahead to the next stage of scrolls study does not mean the abandonment of traditional methods and approaches. There is still a great deal of basic work to be done. Some of the smaller scrolls have only been studied in any depth or details by the editor who prepared them for the *DJD* edition; no matter how well this initial work was done, it can profit by another eye, another set of questions. Publications that were done very early on – for example, the first volume of cave 4 materials that John Allegro made available to the waiting public quickly by 1966 – now call for re-edition with greater care and in light of what we have learned in the last 40 years.[6] Above all, we need to return to the major 'big scrolls' from cave 1 that have been so influential in shaping our understanding, and restudy them in light of the multiple – and very divergent – copies that we now have from all the other caves. It is clear that each one of these basic texts, the *Rule of the Community*, the *Thanksgiving Psalms*, the *War Scroll*, is a much more complex document than first assumed and went through complex processes of redaction and revision. Given that scholars have worked literally for hundreds of years on the formation of the four Christian gospels and the relationships between them, it is not so surprising that after 50 we do not have answers yet for basic questions about the formation and redaction history of the key documents of the Essene community!

In the light of such further study of both key sources and smaller documents we can return again to some of the fundamental questions that faced the first generation of scholars. What sociological model should we use for describing the community that produced the scrolls: that of a sect? A voluntary association? Are the authors of the scrolls to be identified with the Essenes of Philo, Josephus and Pliny? Can we say any more more about the identity of the Teacher of Righteousness? What is the relationship of these people to other Jewish groups: the Pharisees? The temple? The 'Jesus Movement'? The early church of Jerusalem? After 50 years, these are still real questions, and the last word has not been said on any of them.

But after half a decade where textual, philological and historical scholars carried most of the burden, it is now the time for drawing other scholars and resources into the study of the scrolls. On the one hand, there is still much that the 'hard scientists', working in specialties as diverse and complex as AMS (accelerator mass spectography), archeobotany, DNA analysis and INAA (instrumental neutron activation analysis) can contribute to issues of dating, the technical preparation of the animal skins, the origin of the clay used in the making of pottery and so on. In addition, new advances in photography and electronic imaging have already proven to have the potential to enable us to read at least some letters, words and lines that have previously been totally inscrutable – and so far only a handful of scrolls have been re-studied with this technology. But equally exciting is what scholars who are trained in various humanistic and social scientific methodologies and disciplines might contribute. Now that the texts are accessible, they can be read by a sociologist of deviant groups, a Bakhtinian literary critic, a rhetorician and specialist in communication theory, someone trained in ritual studies. Drawing upon a wider variety of specialties with a more interdisciplinary perspective will cause the scrolls to be read in new ways that will generate new questions and, almost certainly, new issues and problems to be considered.

I want to end by recalling the words of one of the key figures of the first generation, Père Roland de Vaux, who was so intensely involved in both the publication and the archaeology of those early years. De Vaux often said, 'What I learn today I will teach today; what I learn tomorrow I will teach tomorrow.' The same can be said about the state of scholarship on the Dead Sea Scrolls today. We have learned much from the scrolls in the past 50 years, but there is still much more to be learned from this 'absolutely incredible find'.

## Notes

1. See the list in note 1, p. xvii.
2. For this major work of consolidation Lawrence H. Schiffman and James C. VanderKam were the Editors-in-chief, along with Editors (George J. Brooke, John J. Collins, Florentino García Martínez, Eileen M. Schuller, Emanuel Tov, Eugene Ulrich) and over 150 other contributors.
3. Readers who are looking for further more specialized but still accessible studies can turn to the following series that are currently in process: George J. Brooke (ed.), *Literature of the Dead Sea Scrolls*, from

# Looking to the Future

Routledge Press (three volumes are already published: Daniel J. Harrington, *Wisdom Texts from Qumran*; John J. Collins, *Apocalypticism in the Dead Sea Scrolls*; James C. VanderKam, *Calendars in the Dead Sea Scrolls*); Philip Davies (ed.), *Companion to the Qumran Scrolls*, from Continuum (six volumes are in print: Timothy Lim, *Pesharim*; Hannah Harrington, *The Purity Texts*; Jonathan Campbell, *The Exegetical Texts*; Jean Duharme, *The War Texts*; Charlotte Hempel, *The Damascus Texts*; Sidnie White Crawford, *The Temple Scroll and Related Texts*); and Martin G. Abegg and Peter W. Flint (eds), *Commentaries on the Dead Sea Scrolls*, from Eerdmans (one volume now available: James R. Davila, *Liturgical Works*).

4. Martin G. Abegg with James Bowley and Edward Cook, in consultation with Emanuel Tov, *The Dead Sea Scrolls Concordance: The Non-Biblical Texts from Qumran*.

5. A number of volumes on texts from the Dead Sea Scrolls are in progress but none have been published yet by Fortress Press.

6. A re-edition of John Allegro's volume V of *Discoveries in the Judaean Desert* is currently being prepared by George J. Brooke and Moshe Bernstein.

# Select Bibliography

These pages give full bibliographic information for books and chapters mentioned in the Notes to each chapter.

Martin G. Abegg, Peter W. Flint and Eugene Ulrich, 1999, *The Dead Sea Scrolls Bible: The Oldest Known Bible Translated for the First Time into English*, San Francisco: Harper.

Martin G. Abegg with James Bowley and Edward Cook, 2003, *The Dead Sea Scrolls Concordance: Volume One, The Non-Biblical Texts from Qumran*, Parts One and Two, Leiden: Brill.

Léonie R. Archer, 1989, *Her Price Is Beyond Rubies: The Jewish Woman in Greco-Roman Palestine*, Sheffield: Sheffield Academic Press.

Nahman Avigad and Yigael Yadin, 1956, *A Genesis Apocryphon: A Scroll from the Wilderness of Judaea*, Jerusalem: Magnes Press and Heikhal Ha-Sefer.

Michael Baigent and Richard Leigh, 1991, *The Dead Sea Scrolls Deception*, London: Corgi Books.

Christopher Burchard, 1957, *Bibliographie zu den Handschriften von Toten Meer*, Berlin: Alfred Töpelmann.

R. H. Charles, 1913, *The Apocrypha and Pseudepigrapha of the Old Testament in English*, 2 volumes, Oxford: Oxford University Press.

# Select Bibliography

James, H. Charlesworth (ed.), 1972, *John and Qumran*, London: Geoffrey Chapman.

John J. Collins, 1997, *Apocalypticism in the Dead Sea Scrolls*, The Literature of the Dead Sea Scrolls Series, London: Routledge.

Frank Moore Cross, 1995, *The Ancient Library of Qumran*, rev edn (first edn, 1958), Minneapolis: Fortress Press.

Frank Moore Cross, 1965, 'The Development of the Jewish Scripts' in G. Ernest Wright (ed.), *The Bible and the Ancient Near East: Essays in Honor of William Foxwell Albright*, Garden City, NY: Doubleday, pp. 133–202.

James R. Davila, 2000, *Liturgical Works*, Eerdman's Commentaries on the Dead Sea Scrolls, Grand Rapids: Eerdmans.

Devorah Dimant, 1997, 'The Scrolls and the Study of Early Judaism' in Robert A. Kugler and Eileen M. Schuller (eds), *The Dead Sea Scrolls at Fifty: Proceedings of the 1997 Society of Biblical Literature Qumran Section Meetings*, pp. 43–60.

Robert Donceel and Pauline Donceel-Voûte, 1994, 'The Archaeology of Khirbet Qumran' in Michael O. Wise et al. (eds), *Methods of Investigation of the Dead Sea Scrolls and the Khirbet Qumran Site*, New York: New York Academy of Sciences.

Robert Eisenman, 1983, *Maccabees, Zadokites, Christians and Qumran*, Leiden: E. J. Brill

Robert Eisenman, 1986, *James the Just in the Habakkuk Pesher*, Leiden: E. J. Brill.

Daniel Falk, 1998, *Daily Sabbath and Festival Prayers in the Dead Sea Scrolls*, Leiden: Brill.

Edward D. Herbert and Emanuel Tov, 2002, *The Bible as Book: The Hebrew Bible and the Judaean Desert Discoveries*, London: The British Library and Oak Knoll Press.

Lawrence A. Hoffman, 1979, *The Canonization of the Synagogue Service*, Notre Dame: University of Notre Dame Press.

# The Dead Sea Scrolls

Jean-Baptiste Humbert and Alain Chambon, 1994, *Fouilles de Khirbet Qumrân et de Aïn Feshkha*, in Volume I: Album de photographies; Répetoire du fonds photographique; Synthèse des notes de chantier du Père Roland de Vaux OP. Volume II: Studies of Anthropology, Physics and Chemistry, Göttingen: Vandenhoeck & Ruprecht, 2003, English edn trans. and revised by Stephen J. Pfann, 2003.

Tal Ilan, 1995, *Jewish Women and Greco-Roman Palestine: An Inquiry into Image and Status*, Tübingen: J. C. B. Mohr (Paul Siebeck).

John S. Kloppenborg, and Stephen G. Wilson (eds), 1996, *Voluntary Associations in the Graeco-Roman World*, London: Routledge.

Robert A. Kugler and Eileen Schuller (eds), 1999, *The Dead Sea Scrolls at Fifty: Proceedings of the 1997 Society of Biblical Literature Qumran Section Meetings*, Atlanta: Scholars Press.

Jodi Magness, 2002, *The Archaeology of Qumran and the Dead Sea Scrolls*, Grand Rapids: Eerdmans.

Florentino García Martínez, 1988, *The Dead Sea Scrolls Translated*, Grand Rapids: Eerdmans.

Florentino García Martínez and Eibert Tigchelaar, 1999, *The Dead Sea Scrolls Study Edition*, two volumes, Grand Rapids: Eerdmans (texts in English and Hebrew).

Florentino García Martínez and Donald W. Parry, 1996, *A Bibliography of the Finds in the Desert of Judah 1970–1995*, Leiden: E. J. Brill.

J. T. Milik, 1959, *Ten Years of Discovery in the Wilderness of Judea*, trans. John Strugnell, London: SCM Press.

J. T. Milik in collaboration with Matthew Black, 1976, *The Books of Enoch: Aramaic Fragments of Qumran Cave 4*, Oxford: Clarendon Press.

Jerome Murphy O'Connor (ed.), 1968, *Paul and Qumran: Studies in New Testament Exegesis*, London: Geoffrey Chapman.

# Select Bibliography

Carol Newsom, 1985, *Songs of the Sabbath Sacrifice: A Critical Edition*, Harvard Semitic Studies, Atlanta: Scholars Press.

Carol Newsom, 1990, '"Sectually Explicit" Literature from Qumran' in William Propp, Baruch Halpern and David Noel Freedman (eds), *The Hebrew Bible and Its Interpreters*, Winona Lake, IN: Eisenbrauns.

Bilhah Nitzan, 1994, *Qumran Prayer and Religious Poetry*, Leiden: Brill.

Avital Pinnick, 2001, *The Orion Center Bibliography of the Dead Sea Scrolls (1995–2000)*, Leiden: Brill.

Elisha Qimron and John Strugnell, 1985, 'An Unpublished Halakhic Letter from Qumran' in *Biblical Archaeology Today: Proceedings of the International Congress on Biblical Archaeology Jerusalem, April 1984*, Jerusalem: Israel Exploration Society, pp. 400–7.

Chaim Rabin, 1958, *The Zadokite Documents*, Oxford: Clarendon Press.

Mar Athanasius Y. Samuel, 1966, *The Treasure of Qumran, My Story of the Dead Sea Scrolls*, Philadelphia: Westminster Press.

Lawrence H. Schiffman, 1995, *Reclaiming the Dead Sea Scrolls*, Anchor Bible Reference Library, New York: Doubleday.

Lawrence H. Schiffman and James C. VanderKam (eds), 2000, *Encyclopedia of the Dead Sea Scrolls*, 2 volumes, New York: Oxford University Press.

Lawrence H. Schiffman, Emanuel Tov and James C. VanderKam (eds), 2000, *The Dead Sea Scrolls Fifty Years After Their Discovery 1947–1997*, Jerusalem: Israel Exploration Society in cooperation with the Shrine of the Book, Israel Museum.

Eileen M. Schuller, 1986, *Non-Canonical Psalms from Qumran: A Pseudepigraphic Collection*, Harvard Semitic Studies, Atlanta: Scholars Press.

Eileen M. Schuller, 1990, 'Some Observations on Blessings of God in Texts from Qumran' in Harold W. Attridge, John J.

Collins, Thomas H. Tobin (eds), *Of Scribes and Scrolls: Studies on the Hebrew Bible, Intertestamental Judaism and Christian Origins Presented to John Strugnell*, Lanham: University Press of America, pp. 133–44.

Eileen M. Schuller, 2000, 'Petitionary Prayer and the Religion of Qumran' in John J. Collins and Robert A. Kugler (eds), *Religion in the Dead Sea Scrolls*, Grand Rapids: Eerdmans, pp. 29–45.

Hershel Shanks, 1994, *Frank Moore Cross: Conversations with a Bible Scholar*, Washington: Biblical Archaeological Society.

Neil Asher Silberman, 1994, *The Hidden Scrolls: Christianity, Judaism and the War for the Dead Sea Scrolls*, New York: G. P. Putnam's Sons.

Hartmut Stegemann, 1998, *The Library of Qumran: On the Essenes, Qumran, John the Baptist and Jesus*, Grand Rapids: Eerdmans.

Krister Stendahl, 1957, *The Scrolls and the New Testament*, New York: Harper (reissued by Crossroad Press, 1992).

Eleazar L. Sukenik, 1954, *The Treasure of the Hidden Scrolls of the Hebrew University* (in Hebrew); 1955, *The Dead Sea Scrolls of the Hebrew University* (in English), Jerusalem: Magnes Press.

Carsten Peter Thiede, 1992, *The Earliest Gospel Manuscript? The Qumran Papyrus 7Q5 and its Significance for New Testament Studies*, London: Paternoster Press.

Emanuel Tov, 2002, 'The Biblical Texts from the Judean Desert – An Overview and Analysis of the Published Texts' in Edward D. Herbert and Emanuel Tov (eds), *The Bible as Book: The Hebrew Bible and the Judaean Desert Discoveries*, Leiden: Brill, pp. 139–66.

John C. Trever, 1977, *The Untold Story of Qumran*, Westwood, NJ: F. R. Revell.

Eugene Ulrich, 2001, 'The Bible in the Making: The Scriptures

# Select Bibliography

Found at Qumran' in Peter W. Flint (ed.), *The Bible at Qumran: Text, Shape and Interpretation*, Grand Rapids: Eerdmans, pp. 51–66.

James C. VanderKam, 1994, *The Dead Sea Scrolls Today*, Grand Rapids: Eerdmans.

James C. VanderKam and Peter Flint, 2002, *The Meaning of the Dead Sea Scrolls: The Significance for Understanding the Bible, Judaism, Jesus and Christianity*, San Francisco: Harper.

Roland de Vaux, 1973, *Archaeology and the Dead Sea Scrolls*, London: Oxford University Press.

Geza Vermes, 1977, *The Dead Sea Scrolls: Qumran in Perspective*, Cleveland: Collins & World.

Geza Vermes, 1997, *The Complete Dead Sea Scrolls in English*, Harmondsworth: Penguin.

Geza Vermes, 1999, *An Introduction to the Complete Dead Sea Scrolls*, Minneapolis: Fortress.

Geza Vermes and Martin D. Goodman (eds), 1989, *The Essenes According to the Classical Sources*, Sheffield: JSOT Press.

Eric Werner, 1970, *The Sacred Bridge: Liturgical Parallels in the Synagogue and the Early Church*, New York: Schocken Books.

Edmund Wilson, 1971, *The Dead Sea Scrolls 1947–1969*, Collins, Fontana Library.

Michael O. Wise, Martin G. Abegg, Edward Cook, 1996, 2005, *The Dead Sea Scrolls: A New Translation*, San Francisco: HarperCollins.

Yigael Yadin, 1957, *The Message of the Scrolls*, New York: Simon and Shuster.

Yigael Yadin, 1983, *The Temple Scroll,* 3 volumes, Jerusalem: Israel Exploration Society.

## Media Resources

***Microfiche of Photos***: Photos of all the fragments and many photos of the site are available on microfiche, Emanuel Tov with Stephen J. Pfann, 1993, *The Dead Sea Scrolls on Microfiche: A Comprehensive Facsimile Edition of the Texts from the Judaean Desert*, Leiden: E. J. Brill; and on CD-ROM *The Dead Sea Scrolls Electronic Reference Library* from Brill (1999). A collection of the photos of John Allegro has been edited by George J. Brooke, *The Allegro Qumran Photo Collection*, Leiden: Brill, 1996.

***Orion Center Website***: The Orion Center at Hebrew University, Jerusalem, has a large web site with a wealth of material. Some of it is geared to a more specialized audience, but there are well-marked sections for the general reader. Each week a bibliography of new books and articles is added: http://orion.mscc.huji.ac.il.

***Shrine of the Book, Israel Museum, Jerusalem***: a website for the general reader: http://www.imj.org.il/eng/shrine.

# John Albert Hall

Churchman, chemist, pioneer, soldier, businessman and philanthropist, John Albert Hall (1869–1933) emigrated from Britain to Canada in the last decade of the nineteenth century, and made his home in Victoria, British Columbia. He left a legacy to the Diocese of British Columbia to found a lectureship to stimulate harmony between Christian religion and contemporary thought. Colonel Hall's generosity sustained the work of three successive Canon Lecturers: Michael Coleman, Hilary Butler and Thomas Bailey. It also helped found the Greater Victoria Lay School of Theology. Since 1995, it has supported an annual lectureship programme at the University of Victoria's Centre for Studies in Religion and Society.

The Centre for Studies in Religion and Society was established in 1991 to foster the scholarly study of religion in relation to any and all aspects of culture and society, both contemporary and historical. Through its publications, fellowships, interdisciplinary research networks and public education programmes, the CSRS provides a rich learning environment for many within the university and beyond.

John Albert Hall lecturers are outstanding scholars of Christianity who address themselves to the church, the university and the community during a two-week fellowship in Victoria, Canada. Publication of these lectures allows a wider audience to benefit from both the John Albert Hall legacy and the work of the CSRS.

# Index of Names and Subjects

# Index of Names and Subjects